Introduction

The Tennessee Centennial Exposition was held in Nashville in 1897 to celebrate Tennessee's one-hundredth anniversary of statehood (the state's centennial was actually 1896). Modeled after the Chicago Columbian Exposition in 1893, it featured exhibitions on the industry, agriculture, commerce, and transportation of the state as well as displays on the educational and cultural achievements.

The Woman's Building featured displays of domestic arts and home economics. As part of the exposition, Mollie Huggins compiled a cookbook called *Tried and True: Tennessee Model Household Guide*. Carrie McGavock submitted eight recipes for inclusion in the cookbook, all of which are reproduced in this volume.

The well-known Nashville landmark The Parthenon in Centennial Park is the only building still standing on the site where it was originally built for the exposition. The Knights of Pythias building was disassembled several years after the exposition and moved to a hill west of Franklin where it is today a private home.

Right, Carnton as seen today.

View from the Porch

A Collection of Recipes from
Friends of Carnton Plantation

Conceived, compiled and edited by Margie Thessin

Assisted by Becky Barkley, Lisa Patton, Margaret Roberts, Joanna
Stephens, Elizabeth Stout and Katie Tate

Special Thanks to Robert Hicks

And everyone who generously contributed their favorite recipes

December, 2008

Cover design: Andy Mangrum
Interior design: Margie Thessin

All proceeds from the sale of this book will go to the preservation and operation of Historic Carnton Plantation.

Photo credits:

Cover photos: Bruce Wolf
Page 4: Joanna Stephens
Pages 13, 41, 107, 122, 136: Bruce Wolf
Pages 53, 65: John Chastain
Page 131: Eric A. Jacobson
Pages 11, 17, 19, 21, 29, 39, 52, 64, 73, 78, 85, 93 101: Carnton archives

ISBN: 1440469520

EAN-13 is 9781440469527

Carnton is a national model dedicated to the preservation, interpretation and management of a Franklin, Tennessee house museum, historic landscape and Civil War battle site. We communicate the compelling story of how the Battle of Franklin and Reconstruction impacted and changed the families of the McGavock Plantation in the 19th century.

Contents

Foreword

Southerners like to eat. It's just one of those facts that can neither be refuted nor denied. I'm living proof of this, as were my ancestors before me.

Our Southern cuisine was born out of the convergence of the Scots-Irish and the West Africans in this new world. Or, at least, that's my story.

Of course there were many other ingredients that went into the mix, like the massive variety of new foods that were native to this place, not to mention the impact of the French and the Germans. But all and all, it was the convergence of the Scots-Irish and the West Africans that gave us our wonderfully rich, unhealthy fare that we call home cooking. Can you imagine what it must have been like the first time a Scots-Irishman, raised on boiled meat, boiled roots, oats and barley sank his teeth into the fried delicacies of West Africa? He must have truly believed that he had died and gone to heaven.

For just as the Portuguese took the art of deep-frying along the trade route from West Africa to Japan and gave the Far East tempura, so the enslaved West Africans gave the South the fundamentals of our cooking. The irony may be that while we thankfully lost 'The War' and out of it became Americans, our cooking has triumphed over all the rest. A friend who lives in China reports that the largest franchise restaurant in China today is KFC. This makes me smile when I think of our family's cook, Minnie Nichols' pride in her fried chicken and chess pies.

Carrie McGavock and her family were no strangers to good food. A visiting cousin, writing back to the McGavocks of Southwest Virginia, remarked that Carrie still set the best table of anyone in their extended family of cooks across Virginia and Tennessee.

So it's appropriate that we who love this place, this hallowed ground called Carnton, would want to continue the tradition laid down by Carrie and Mariah Reddick and our own ancestors, both black and white, and put together this offering of recipes. While the kitchen at Carnton disappeared in the tornado of 1909, through these offerings, its smells and the smells of kitchens throughout our land are passed on to another generation, into another century. These are not simply recipes. You hold in your hands our families' treasures and a big piece of our legacy.

After grace is said, eat up!

Robert Hicks

Mariah Reddick is holding Carrie Winder Cowan, Carrie McGavock's granddaughter by her daughter Hattie, January 6, 1886.

Recipes

The family's cruet set rests on the mixing table in the Carnton dining room.

Beverages

Mixing tables were a popular addition to dining rooms in the 19th century. There is one in the Carnton dining room today. From this table, alcoholic beverages would be served to guests.

Eggnog was a special drink, particularly during the Christmas holidays. The gentlemen would enjoy the whisky-laced eggnog, while ladies and children would be served the non-alcoholic version; another drink called Syllabub would be enjoyed during the season as well.

EGGNOG

12 eggs, separated
1 cup sugar
1 cup milk

2 cups whiskey
6 cups heavy cream
Nutmeg

Separate the eggs and stir yolks till well blended. Whip the egg whites till stiff and then whip the cream. Add everything together, except the nutmeg. Chill overnight. When serving, grate the nutmeg atop the eggnog in the glass. Makes about a half gallon or so.

SYLLABUB

3 cups apple juice
¼ cup lemon juice
1 tsp. light corn syrup
3 Tbsp. grated lemon rind

2 egg whites
¼ cup sugar
2 cups milk
1 cup light cream

Mix apple juice, lemon juice, corn syrup and grated lemon rind in large bowl. Stir until sugar dissolves. Refrigerate until cold. Just before serving, beat egg whites until foamy; then beat in ¼ cup sugar, one tablespoon at a time, until meringue peaks. Beat into cider mixture milk and light cream, beating until frothy. Pour into punch bowl. Spoon meringue in small puffs on top and sprinkle with nutmeg.

HOT GRAPE JUICE

Concord grapes grow prolifically on the cedar arbor in Carnton's garden. Perhaps the McGavocks enjoyed the grapes in this form.

1 pt. grape juice
1 cup hot water
Juice of one lemon
1 stick cinnamon
3 cloves
Sugar to taste

Mix together and serve hot.

Hattie McGavock Ayres

DANNY ANDERSON'S GENTLEMAN JACK CARNTON MINT JULEP

Danny, a past Carnton president and long-time supporter, is the king of the Mint Julep. Danny reports the drink is best enjoyed on Carnton's back porch, in a rocker, at sunset!

Water
Sugar
Crushed ice
Fresh mint from the Carnton garden
Jack Daniel's Tennessee Whiskey

Mix equal parts sugar and water, stir and cook to thicken a few minutes. Toss in a few sprigs of mint as the syrup cools to infuse the mint, but remove it before using because it will turn dark. Place one teaspoon of syrup in the bottom of an 8 ounce glass. Fill with ice. Fill with Gentleman Jack. Add mint sprig. This is a very strong drink so you may want to add more of the sugar and water mixture.

Danny Anderson

MULLED CIDER

A modern adaptation of a c. 1855 West Tennessee recipe

1 gallon unfiltered apple cider
½ cup brown sugar
½ cup lemon juice (fresh or from concentrate)
3 sticks cinnamon
8 whole cloves and 1 teaspoon of dried orange peel, all tied up in a bag.

Slice a whole orange and a whole lemon. Simmer all ingredients for an hour or more. Then add 2 cups of apple brandy and serve.

Robert Hicks

WASSAIL TEA

Traditionally served at Christmas, wassail dates back to the Middle Ages. The modern version bears no resemblance to the historic one. Here's the old English drinking song:

Wassail! wassail! All over the town;
Our toast it is white and our ale it is brown;
Our bowl it is made of the white maple tree;
With the wassailing bowl, we'll drink to thee.

1 cup granulated sugar
½ cup packed brown sugar
4 cups apple cider
1 stick cinnamon
12 whole cloves

2 cups orange juice
2 cups grapefruit juice
Orange slices
Maraschino cherry halves
Whole cloves

In large saucepan combine granulated sugar, brown sugar, and apple cider; boil, stirring until sugar dissolves. Add cinnamon stick and cloves. Reduce heat; simmer 5 minutes. Add grapefruit and orange juice. Heat, but do not boil. Strain. Serve in heat-proof mugs with orange slices decorated with maraschino cherry halves and whole cloves.

Marilyn Lehew

16

Randal McGavock was born in Virginia, served as the mayor of Nashville, and built Carnton in 1826.

Sarah Rodgers and Randal McGavock married in 1811.

PLANTATION TEA

1 qt. boiling water
7 tea bags
12 sprigs mint
1 cup sugar
1 - 6 oz. can frozen lemonade concentrate

4 lemonade cans of water
1 ½ cups pineapple juice
Crushed ice
Sprigs of fresh mint

In large bowl or pitcher pour boiling water over tea bags, mint and sugar. Stir. Let sit for 30 minutes, then discard tea bags and mint, squeezing them out into liquid. Add lemonade, water and pineapple juice. Chill to serve. Serve over crushed ice with a sprig of fresh mint in each glass. Yield: ½ gallon.

Beverly Jenkins

GRANDMA ADELE'S FROZEN MARGARITAS

3 - 6 oz. cans frozen lemonade
3 - 6 oz. cans frozen limeade
5 - 6 oz. cans water
12 oz. tequila
6 oz. triple sec

Freeze for 2 - 3 days. Stir and serve. Will keep for months.

Jenni Peterson

FRUIT TEA

6 small tea bags
4 cups boiling water
1 ½ cups sugar
1 - 6 oz. can frozen concentrate
orange juice

1 - 6 oz. can frozen concentrate
lemonade
10 cups water

Place tea bags in boiling water. Let steep 5 minutes. Add sugar, stir until dissolved. Add remaining ingredients. Stir until well mixed.
(May also substitute Orange-Pineapple-Banana Concentrate for one of the cans as well)
Yield: 1 gallon.

Nena Manci

PEARL'S PUNCH

3 liters Chablis
46 oz. can pineapple juice
4 cups orange juice
2 cups lemon juice

¾ cup strawberry syrup
3 cups simple syrup (3 cups hot water mixed with 3 cups Splenda or sugar)

Mix all ingredients. Serve over ice.

Ginny Holley

CHRISTY CLARK'S PERKED PUNCH

3 cups unsweetened pineapple
juice
3 cups cranberry juice
1½ cups water

⅓ cup brown sugar or 4 packets
of Sweet-n-Low
1½ tsp. whole cloves
1 cinnamon stick
⅛ tsp. salt

Pour juices into percolator, and put all the spices in the basket. Allow to
perk a full cycle.

Ginny Holley

*Sarah Rodgers and
Randal McGavock
had seven children. John
was the third oldest, and
lived the longest.*

*Sarah was the sister-in-
law of Felix Grundy and
a friend of Rachel
Jackson.*

ICE CREAM PUNCH

Perfect for the traditional wedding reception of cake, punch, nuts and mints, this recipe is from the Choices Restaurant cookbook. Choices Restaurant was located at the corner of Fourth Avenue and Main Street and was a favorite of Franklin residents for many years.

3 - 46 oz. cans pineapple juice
3 - 12 oz. cans frozen orange
juice concentrate, mix according
to directions
2 - 12 oz. cans frozen lemonade
concentrate, mix according to
direction

1 - 46 oz. can or equivalent
apricot nectar
2 qts. ginger ale
3 qts. 7 Up
3 gallons vanilla ice cream
(mashed with potato masher)
Yellow food coloring, optional

Add a few drops yellow food coloring to mashed ice cream, if desired. Add fruit juices to ice cream. At serving time add ginger ale and 7 Up.

Marilyn Lehew

COFFEE ICE CREAM PUNCH

My grandmother and her sister loved to have their Sunday school class over to their home for luncheons. I remember as a little girl, Grandmama Frances sneaking me a cup of this delicious concoction and especially her whispering in my ear not to tell my daddy because it had coffee in it.

1 qt. vanilla ice cream
3 cups milk
¼ cup sugar
1 tsp. vanilla
¼ tsp. nutmeg

6 cups freshly brewed coffee,
cooled
Coffee ice cubes
Whipped cream

Spoon ice cream by tablespoons into a punch bowl. Add milk, sugar, vanilla, and nutmeg. Sir until combined. Stir in coffee and ice cubes. Ladle into cups. Garnish with whipped cream. Serve right away. Makes 24 (4 ounce) servings.

Lisa Patton

Carrie Winder's portrait was painted by Washington Cooper and hangs at Carnton today. She married John McGavock in 1848 and bore him five children.

Appetizers

Small tastings now known as appetizers, hors d'oeuvres and canapés were rarely served in 19th century America. Although the concept of presenting a variety of nibbles preparatory to a meal dates back to ancient upper-class Greeks and Romans, the cocktail party or like gathering serving what we now call appetizers really came into its own in the 20th century. Now it's hard to imagine a football game, Christmas party or pool party without our favorites such as artichoke dip, guacamole, stuffed mushrooms and salsa!

CARNTON PICKLES

The recipe has been attributed to Miss Louise Winder and was sent to Carnton in 1979 by Susan James, who found it in a cookbook entitled De Bonnes Choses A Manger (Good Things to Eat), *published by St. Matthews Guild, Houma, Louisiana, 5th ed., 1945. Louise was Carrie's sister.*

1 gallon chopped cabbage	2 pounds sugar
½ gallon chopped green tomatoes	1 oz. cloves
	1 oz. cinnamon
1 pt. chopped bell peppers	1 oz. allspice
1 qt. chopped onions	1 oz. celery seed
¼ pt. chopped horseradish	Vinegar, salt and pepper to taste

Mix well together, sprinkle with salt, let hang overnight in a thin bag, next morning scald and squeeze dry. Add sugar, spices, and celery seed. Salt and pepper to taste. Cover well with vinegar. Boil until vegetables are tender, seal hot.

Miss Louise Winder

DIDEE DIP

Carrie Winder had Tennessee roots, but lived in Louisiana at the time of her marriage to John McGavock. Board member Becky Barkley, like Carrie a Louisiana girl, presents this recipe in honor of her and Carrie's home state. Becky notes that this dip is especially popular on New Year's Eve.

½ stick butter
2 can black-eyed peas
2 jalapeno peppers
½ lb. sharp cheddar cheese
2 pods garlic, minced
½ chopped onion

Heat all ingredients except cheese. Then put in blender and heat up again and add cheese. Serve hot with Doritos. Freezes well.

Becky Duke Barkley

SOUTHERN SALSA

The recipe came from a friend in Paris, Tennessee, who said she had never served it that someone didn't ask for the recipe. This has been true for me as well. It is a perfect appetizer in the summer months.

2 cans black-eyed peas, rinsed and drained
1 can shoe peg corn, drained
1 medium onion, chopped
1 medium green pepper, chopped
3 Roma tomatoes, chopped
1 - 8 oz. package of Good Seasons Italian dressing, mixed according to directions
1 jar of red pepper relish

Mix all and chill 6 - 8 hours. Serve with Fritos.

Margaret Roberts

STUFFED MUSHROOMS

Fresh mushrooms
1 lb. of hot sausage
1 - 8 oz. pkg. cream cheese

Wash mushrooms and trim stems. Brown and drain sausage. Add cream cheese. Fill mushrooms with sausage mixture. Broil for 5 minutes. Then bake at 350 degrees for 20 minutes.

Marianne Schroer

BELGIUM ENDIVE APPETIZER

6 oz. goat cheese or bleu cheese
3 Tbsp. or more as needed of
heavy cream
1 scallion minced
1 Tbsp. fresh parsley

⅛ tsp. salt
Pinch of pepper
2 large heads of Belgium endive
¼ cup chopped walnuts

Mix all ingredients together or you can sprinkle walnuts on top. Use about 1½ tablespoons of mixture to fill each leaf of endive. Add more cream if mixture becomes too thick to spread.

Becky Darby

GUACAMOLE

4 avocados (ripe brown)
3 Tbsp. lemon juice
8 dashes Tabasco
½ cup red onion, diced fine
2 large cloves garlic, minced

1 tsp. salt
1 tsp. pepper
1 medium tomato, seeded and
diced in small pieces

Mix all ingredients in bowl except tomato pieces. Cut avocado mixture with two knives until finely diced. Next stir in tomatoes. Serve with tortilla chips.

Lucy Battle

MUSHROOM TURNOVERS

CREAM CHEESE PASTRY

1 cup butter, softened
1 - 8 oz. cream cheese, softened
½ tsp. salt
2 cups flour
2 tsp. milk
1 egg yolk

Mix butter, cream cheese, salt and flour to form soft dough. Chill overnight. Break off part of dough (keeping remainder chilled until time to roll it out) and roll it paper-thin on a floured surface. With cookie cutter cut into 2 inch circles and fill with mushroom filling.

When ready to cook brush tops with egg yolk beaten with milk. Place on ungreased baking sheet and cook at 350 degrees for 20 minutes. The unbaked pastries may be frozen and baked frozen or thawed slightly.

MUSHROOM FILLING

½ cup fresh mushrooms chopped fine
Dash nutmeg
2 Tbsp. butter
1 tsp. lemon juice
½ cup chopped onion

2 tsp. flour
½ tsp. salt
½ cup sour cream
Dash white pepper
1 tsp. dill weed

Sauté mushrooms in butter with the onion until limp. Add salt, pepper, nutmeg and lemon juice. Blend in flour until smooth and slightly thickened. Stir in sour cream and dill weed. Cool filling. Place small amount of filling on one side of pastry round. Fold over and crimp edges with fork tines. Makes about 4 dozen.

Anne Rutherford

PARTY CHEESE BALL

2 - 8 oz. pkg. cream cheese
1 - 8 ½ oz. can crushed
pineapple, drained
¼ cup green pepper, minced or
finely chopped

2 Tbsp. green onions, finely
chopped
1 tsp. seasoned salt
1 cup finely chopped nuts (to
roll ball in)

Mix cheese and pineapple. Add other ingredients. Chill until firm
enough to roll in nuts.

Serve with variety crackers.

Nena Manci

CHRISTMAS CHEESE BALL

*I have made this recipe for Christmas for 30 plus years. The logs make great hostess
gifts when invited to parties or teacher gifts. The red pimento and green peppers look
pretty at Christmas!*

2 - 8 oz. pkgs. cream cheese
1 Tbsp. chopped pimento
1 Tbsp. chopped green pepper
1 small onion, grated
2 tsp. Worcestershire sauce
Dash of Tabasco
Pecans, finely chopped
Dash of garlic

Combine all except nuts and mix well. Chill. Shape into a ball and roll in
nuts. Can also shape into 3 logs.

Serve on tray with crackers.

Joyce Crutcher

HONEY MUSTARD BRIE

1 - 15 oz. round of Brie
¼ cup honey mustard
½ cup sliced almonds or chopped pecans, toasted
3 - 4 bacon slices, cooked and crumbled

Trim top rind from Brie, cutting to within ½ inch from edges. Place Brie on a baking sheet; spread evenly with mustard, and sprinkle with toasted nuts and bacon. Bake at 325 degrees for 15 - 20 minutes or until Brie is thoroughly heated. Serve with toasted baguettes slices or assorted crackers.

Nancy Moody

ARTICHOKE CRAB DIP

1 cup Parmesan cheese
1 cup mayonnaise
1 cup mozzarella cheese

1 can artichoke hearts, drained
1 can crab meat, drained

Mix all ingredients. Bake 30 minutes.

Carole Guthrie

HUMMUS

8 to 10 cloves garlic, finely chopped
2 - 15 oz. cans cannellini beans
½ cup tahini paste
6 Tbsp. olive oil
¼ cup fresh squeezed lemon juice

1 Tbsp. + ½ tsp. soy sauce
1 tsp. salt
1½ tsp. ground cumin
⅛ tsp. coriander
½ tsp. cayenne pepper
¼ cup cold water

Mix all ingredients together. Chill before serving.

Patti Caprara

STUFFED CELERY

This one and the next are my mother Jean Gould's two favorite appetizers.

Cream cheese
Green olives, chopped
Celery sticks

Mix together cream cheese and olives. Stuff into celery.

CLAM DIP

1- 6 ½ oz. can minced clams, drained
1 - 8 oz. pkg. cream cheese
1 Tbsp. Worcestershire sauce

Dash of garlic salt
Pepper
Fritos corn chips

Mix clams, cream cheese and Worcestershire sauce. Add back about half the liquid. Chill. Serve with Fritos corn chips.

PROSCIUTTO-WRAPPED PICKLES

My mother-in-law Eunice Thessin's favorite easy appetizer. Another easy one!

Baby kosher gherkins
Cream cheese

Prosciutto, cut into 4 x 4 inch squares

Spread cream cheese on prosciutto, wrap pickle.

BACON-WRAPPED WATER CHESTNUTS

Whole water chestnuts
Bacon slices, cut in half

Wrap water chestnuts in bacon, affix with toothpick, broil until bacon cooks thoroughly.

Margie Thessin

John McGavock's portrait hangs in the Carnton dining room over the mantel.

Breads

In the 19th century the average person ate about one pound of bread per day and bread was made daily in every home. The old McGavock kitchen, which was destroyed by a tornado in 1909, more than likely had its own bread oven. A biscuit board was also found in most every kitchen. It was on this table that biscuit dough was prepared, or beaten.

BEATEN BISCUITS

A recipe any cook worth her salt knew by the age of 12. This version was included in the Tennessee Model Household Guide *and credited to "Mrs. C.W. McG, Franklin, Tennessee," as written there.*

1 quart of flour
1 teaspoonful of salt
1 egg
1 tablespoonful of lard
1 tablespoonful of butter

Mix up these ingredients with skimmed milk, work them well together, and beat 15 minutes. Stick with fork and bake quickly.

Carrie McGavock

WAFERS

Here's another offering from the Guide *and credited to Carrie McGavock. Again, as written:*

4 spoonfuls of sugar
4 spoonfuls of flour
4 spoonfuls of cream
1 spoonful of butter

Season to taste with lemon or vanilla. Prepare as for pound cake. Bake in wafer irons, rolling them hot.

Carrie McGavock

FINE EGG BREAD

And another...

One quart of meal, 1 teaspoonful of soda, make stiff with sour milk and thin with warm water, add 2 eggs and then a little salt.

Carrie McGavock

CHEESE MUFFINS

1 - 8 oz. pkg. cream cheese
½ cup margarine
½ cup parmesan cheese
1 tsp. paprika
½ tsp. dried oregano
½ tsp. garlic powder

Mix all ingredients in food processor or mixer. Spread on ½ English muffin. Bake at 375 degrees about 15 minutes or until "puffy." These are good with any soup or chili.

Lynne Davis

CRACKLING BREAD

Lysander McGavock built Midway Plantation, so named because it was located on the pike midway between Nashville and Franklin in Brentwood. Today the property is owned by the Brentwood Country Club. Lysander was John's cousin.

Lysander's daughter Emily married Oliver B. Hayes. Mr. and Mrs. Hayes' son Lysander married Hortense Campbell. McGavock Hayes was one of their sons and the following recipe is from the collection of his wife.

1 cup cracklings	½ tsp. soda
1½ cups corn meal	¼ tsp. salt
¾ cups wheat flour	1 cup sour milk

Mix together and sift the dry ingredients. Add milk; stir in the cracklings. Shape into oblong pones and place in greased baking pan. Bake at 400 degrees for 30 minutes.

Mrs. McGavock Hayes

CONFEDERATE ARTILLERY CORNBREAD

A bang in every bite! This recipe is in memory of my grand-daddy, Pvt. Alexander Campbell (A.C.) Darden, who served in company C, 3rd North Carolina (Light), 1864-65.

2 - 8 ½ oz. pkg. Martha White or Jiffy cornbread/muffin mix	1 - 14 ½ oz. can creamed corn
½ cup vegetable oil	1 ½ cup sour cream
1 medium onion, chopped	4 eggs, beaten
2 cups cheddar cheese, shredded	1 - 10 oz. can Rotel tomatoes, drained, hot or mild

Combine muffin mix and onions, combine remaining ingredients and add to muffin mix/onion. Stir thoroughly until moist. Bake at 350 degrees in a greased 9 x 13 inch pan for 50 - 55 minutes until browned and pulling from sides.

Mercer Darden

RAISIN BRAN MUFFINS

1 - 15 oz. box raisin bran cereal	1 cup vegetable oil
3 cups sugar	2 tsp. vanilla
5 cups flour	1 tsp. cloves
5 tsp. soda	1 tsp. nutmeg
2 tsp. salt	1 tsp. cinnamon
4 beaten eggs	1 quart buttermilk

Mix raisin bran cereal, sugar, flour, soda, salt and spices in a large bowl. Add beaten eggs, oil, vanilla and buttermilk. Mix well and store in refrigerator.

Bake in greased muffin tins at 400 degrees for 15 - 20 minutes. Makes 5 dozen muffins.

Batter keeps several weeks in the refrigerator.

Margaret Roberts

STRAWBERRY BREAD

3 cups flour	4 eggs, well beaten
1 tsp. salt	2 - 10 oz. packages frozen
1 tsp. soda	strawberries, thawed
3 tsp. cinnamon	1¼ cups oil
2 cups sugar	1¼ cups chopped pecans

Sift together dry ingredients in a large bowl and make a well in the center. Mix remaining ingredients and pour into the well. Stir enough to dampen.

Pour into two greased loaf pans. Bake at 350 degrees for 1- 1 ¼ hours. Cool in pans on wire rack 10 minutes, then release from pans and cool completely on wire racks. Recipe can be halved to make one loaf. This bread freezes well.

Rene Evans

CAJUN CORNCAKES

4 cups self-rising flour
8 cups self-rising meal
4 cups sugar
1 large onion, diced

1 medium bell pepper, diced
1 small red pepper, diced
1 gal. buttermilk
1 Tbsp. red pepper flakes

Mix all ingredients together in a large mixing bowl. Form mixture into small cakes. Set grill at 300 degrees and spray non-stick butter onto the griddle. Cook loaves for 2 minutes on each side.

Puckett's Grocery and Restaurant, downtown Franklin and Leiper's Fork

ZUCCHINI LOAVES

3 large eggs, lightly beaten
1 ½ cups sugar
3 cups shredded zucchini (1½ lbs.)
¾ cup vegetable oil
2 tsp. vanilla extract
2 cups all-purpose flour
1 cup whole wheat flour

½ cup wheat germ
¼ cup nonfat dry milk powder
1 tsp. salt
1 tsp. baking soda
1 tsp. baking powder
2 tsp. cinnamon
½ tsp. ground nutmeg
¼ tsp. ground cloves

Combine first five ingredients in a large mixing bowl, stirring well. Combine all-purpose flour and the rest of ingredients in another bowl, stirring well.

Add to the zucchini mixture, stirring just until blended. Spoon batter into two greased and floured 8 x 4 x 2½ inch loaf pans.

Bake at 350 degrees for 45 to 50 minutes or until a wooden pick inserted in the center comes out clean. Cool in pans on a wire rack 10 minutes; remove from pans and cool completely on wire rack.

Rene Evans

REFRIGERATOR ROLLS

I got this recipe from The Belle Meade Mansion Cookbook. *This book went with me to Saudi Arabia. I could only take one book because of the weight restrictions on luggage. The recipes in it used simple ingredients that I knew could be found while there. I did have to alter the recipe a bit – using my method of putting ingredients together as I had learned to make rolls when I was about ten years of age.*

When I returned from Saudi Arabia I shared this recipe with many Franklin friends – I soon became known as "The Roll Queen."

3 ½ cups milk	2 tsp. baking powder
1 cup sugar	1 tsp. soda
1 cup shortening (Crisco)	2 pkg. yeast
8 - 10 cups plain Pillsbury flour	½ cup lukewarm water
1 Tbsp. salt	1 Tbsp. sugar

Heat 1 cup milk with sugar and shortening until they are dissolved. Pour into large mixing bowl and add remaining milk. Mix 3 cups flour, salt, baking powder and soda. Add to milk mixture. Dissolve yeast in lukewarm water to which 1 tablespoon sugar has been added. Add dissolved yeast mixture to milk mixture (make sure water is only lukewarm so that it does not kill the yeast).

Cover and let rise until doubled in bulk. Add enough flour to make soft dough. Place in greased container. Cover dough with oil so it does not become dry, then place in refrigerator.

When ready to bake, take dough from refrigerator and knead. Work as little flour as possible into dough. Roll to ½ inch thickness. Cut into circles and fold in half. Seal half circle with edge of spoon.

Place on a greased sheet and let rise until doubled in bulk. Bake at 375 degrees for 10 - 15 minutes (will keep 8 - 15 days in refrigerator). May also be used for cinnamon rolls, hamburger and hot dog buns. I use a coffee can to cut hamburger buns. Makes 100 rolls.

Joyce Crutcher

BANANA BREAD

I inherited this recipe from a family friend in Atlanta 20 years ago. This truly is a moist bread. You can make use of those over-ripened bananas too!

½ cup oil
1 cup sugar
1 egg
3 very ripe bananas, mashed
3 Tbsp. milk
1 tsp. vanilla
1½ cups all-purpose flour
½ tsp. salt
Nuts (optional)

Add all ingredients together in order. Pour into a greased 9 inch loaf pan. Bake at 350 degrees for 50 - 60 minutes. Cool on a rack.

Tips: I mash the bananas with a fork on wax paper. Sifting the flour gives a better texture.

Bess Kearns

CORN LIGHT BREAD

1½ cups white corn meal
½ cup flour
½ cup sugar
1½ cups buttermilk
½ tsp. baking soda
½ tsp. salt
½ cup melted butter or margarine

Mix all ingredients and let stand 20 minutes, as this makes a finer texture. Pour batter into a greased 8 x 4 inch loaf pan. Bake at 350 degrees for 1 hour.

Lucy Battle

PARMESAN CRESCENTS

2 cups flour
¾ cup soft butter or margarine (do not use light)
2 cups cottage cheese
Dash of salt
1 cup parmesan cheese, divided into fourths

Mix all ingredients well. Separate into fourths; flour hands; roll each section into a ball; wrap in plastic wrap and refrigerate at least one hour. (The dough can also be frozen at this point. When ready to use, thaw completely before rolling out.)

Roll out each ball into an 8 inch circle on a well-floured surface. Sprinkle each circle with ¼ cup parmesan cheese. Cut circle into eight wedges and roll into crescent shapes, beginning at wide end of wedge and rolling in toward the pointed end.

Place on baking sheet and curl edges inward to form crescent shape. Bake at 375 degrees for 20 minutes or until brown. Serve hot.

Rene Evans

SCOTTISH SHORTBREAD

1 lb. butter (no substitutes)
1 cup packed brown sugar
4 - 4 ½ cups all-purpose flour

Cream butter and sugar. Add 3 ¾ cups flour. Mix well. Add enough remaining flour to make a soft non-sticky dough. Divide in half. Roll out on floured surface.

Cut into squares or rectangles. Prick with fork. Bake at 325 degrees about 15 minutes till very lightly browned. Let cool a few minutes before removing from cookie sheet. Sprinkle with sugar.

Deborah Faulkner

MATTIE JACKSON HICKS' SURE
AS GOOD SHORT BREAD

¾ cup softened butter
¼ cup sugar
2 cups of all-purpose flour (not self-rising)

Mix together. If crumbly, blend in 1 to 2 more tablespoons of butter.
Roll out half an inch thick on lightly floured cloth-covered board and cut
into small pieces, 1 x 1 inch. Next punch holes in top of cookies after
placing then on an ungreased cookie sheet. Cook at 350 degrees for
approximately 20 minutes. After 20 minutes they should be very lightly
brown, if not almost white. Remove from sheet and let cool.

Robert Hicks

CLARA MAE GOSEY'S WHOLE-WHEAT
SHORT BISCUITS

*Ms. Gosey was the legendary cook for Miss Ruth Corn and Mrs. Nelson Elam for
many years. Several generations of Williamson Countians were the beneficiaries of
Clara Mae Gosey's whole-wheat short biscuits.*

2 cups stone ground whole-
wheat flour
2 tsp. baking powder
½ tsp. baking soda

½ tsp. salt
¼ cup sugar
½ cup Crisco (shortening)
1 cup buttermilk

In a large mixing bowl combine the whole-wheat flour, sugar, baking
powder, salt and baking soda. Stir until well mixed. Cut in the shortening
until the mixture forms a bowl, kneading if necessary. On a lightly
floured surface, roll the dough to about ½ inch thickness. Cut with a 2
inch biscuit cutter; placing rounds on ungreased baking sheets. Bake in a
400 degree oven about 10 minutes or until the biscuits are golden brown
on the bottom. (Biscuits will be thin and crisp). Serve warm.

Robert Hicks

POPPY SEED BREAD

2 ½ cups granulated sugar
1 ¼ cups oil
3 eggs
3 cups cake flour
1 ½ tsp. baking powder
1 ½ tsp. salt

1 ½ cups whole milk
1 ½ Tbsp. poppy seed
1 ½ tsp. vanilla
1 ½ tsp. almond flavoring
1 ½ tsp. butter flavoring

Cream together sugar, oil and eggs until light and fluffy. Sift together dry ingredients and add to sugar mixture with milk, vanilla, poppy seed and flavorings. Mix well and divide into 2 greased and floured loaf pans and bake at 350 degrees for 35-40 minutes or until done. Top warm bread with glaze.

GLAZE

¼ cup orange juice
¾ cup powdered sugar
½ tsp. vanilla
½ almond flavoring
½ tsp. butter flavoring

Merridee's Breadbasket, Fourth Avenue South, Franklin

When John McGavock died in 1893, the entire town closed for the service at First Presbyterian Church. John received the title "Colonel" when Governor James K. Polk appointed him aide-de-camp in 1840.

SPOON ROLLS

After moving to downtown Franklin in 1977, all of our family enjoyed learning the history of the Battle of Franklin in our own way. We began volunteering with the community organizations that supported Carnton, the Carter House and the Heritage Foundation and our young boys got interested one year in the military reenactments that were part of the downtown Christmas Tour of Homes.

I once came home after the tour to find them asleep on the floor with sheets strung over furniture to make their tents. That experience resulted in the birthday gift of a tent which was the start of several small camping experiences where we learned to enjoy the following recipe. The rolls now continue to be requested when visiting their families.

1 ½ sticks margarine
¼ cup sugar
1 pkg. dry yeast
2 cups very warm water (use ¼ cup of this to dissolve yeast)
1 egg beaten
4 cups self-rising flour

Melt margarine. Mix with sugar and water in large mixing bowl. Add beaten egg, then dissolved yeast. Add flour. Stir until well mixed. Place in airtight bowl in refrigerator. It will keep for about a week.

Drop by spoonfuls in greased miniature or regular muffin tins. Bake in oven at 375 degrees. For regular sized muffins bake for 18 - 20 minutes until lightly browned, 10 - 15 minutes for miniature.

If eating away from home, you can cook ahead and reheat them in wrapped foil.

Gwen King

The cedar grape arbor supports Concord grape vines that produce prolifically. These grapes would have been grown at Carnton in the 19ᵗʰ century.

Soups

During the 19th century, soups and stew were found in every home regardless of wealth. In wealthy homes, soup was merely the first course on the menu of formal dining in the Victorian Era, as reflected in the expression "soup to nuts." For others, soups were often made in large amounts and eaten for both dinner and supper. During the Civil War, when food was scarce, soup was a common staple of a families' diet because it allowed for any leftovers to be reused for "the second time around."

Nowadays, hearty soups satisfy appetites in many homes as the entire evening meal, and soup and salad is a popular luncheon choice.

GUMBO SOUP

Another of Mrs. C.W. McG.'s recipe from the Tennessee Model Household Guide, *here as written:*

One fried chicken, 1 onion, parsley, 1 quart of okra cut up, 1 quart of skinned tomatoes, 1 pint of corn, a few celery leaves. 1 ½ gallons, boil to to ½ gallon. Pepper and salt to taste.

Carrie McGavock

VEGETABLE SOUP

Jacob McGavock Dickinson was a great-nephew of Randal McGavock. He was also the grandson of John Overton of Travelers's Rest. Jacob owned two of Nashville's most storied plantations: first Belle Meade, then he later purchased and brought his grandfather's estate, Traveler's Rest, back into the family. Jacob Dickinson served as Secretary of War under President Howard Taft.

1 soup bone with meat	Fresh or leftover vegetables (3
Celery tops and leaves	cups)
1 onion	1 cup okra, chopped
Water to cover	Tomatoes, chopped
Salt and pepper	1 tsp. cumin

Boil the above for several hours. Drain, saving only the broth, and reheat to boiling. Then add the remaining ingredients.

Mrs. Jacob McGavock Dickinson

BEEF and BLACK BEAN SOUP

1 pound ground chuck	1 cup prepared medium or hot
1 - 12 oz. can black bean soup	chunk salsa
1 - 15 oz. can black beans	¼ cup thinly sliced green onions
rinsed, drained	¼ cup light sour cream
1 ⅓ cup water	4 corn muffins warmed

Brown beef until beef is no longer pink and then pour off drippings. Stir in black bean soup, black beans, water and salsa. Bring to a boil, reduce heat to low. Simmer, uncovered, 15 minutes. Stir in green onions. Remove from heat. Garnish with sour cream. Serve with corn muffins.

If you use Progresso bean soup, cut down on the water. I use Campbell's if I can find it because you add water to it. However, you can't mess it up!

Anne Rutherford

AWFULLY GOOD EPIPHANY NIGHT BEAN SOUP

The first account of this soup being served on Epiphany Night in the Hicks family was mentioned in a letter in 1876 though the tradition and legend of serving bean soup on Epiphany Night goes back to The Wise Men. Throughout my childhood, my grandmother's cook, Minnie Nichols, always started the soup on January 5th, the night before Epiphany, to be served the next evening. In those days, she made heaping amounts for the twenty or so that gathered at my grandmother's on Epiphany Night.

Whatever wasn't devoured that night was warmed over in the days to come by Minnie until the last of it disappeared. My mother adjusted the recipe, cutting many of the steps out when she discovered canned Rotel tomatoes in the 1960s and altered it to serve six.

2 cups of mixed dry beans*
2 qt. water
1 large onion, chopped
1 garlic clove, minced
½ tsp. of salt
1 - 16 oz. can tomatoes, undrained and chopped
1 - 10 oz. can Rotel tomatoes, undrained
1 - 10 oz. can green chilies, undrained

*Use a mix of black beans, black-eyed peas, navy beans, lima beans, red beans, pinto beans, split peas and great Southern beans-- as our family called them.

Wash and 'look' the beans over the night of January 5th. Place in a large pot with a lid. Cover with water 2 inches above beans. Let soak overnight. Drain and add 2 quarts of water, onion, garlic and salt.

Simmer 1 ¼ hours or until tender. Add canned tomatoes, Rotel tomatoes and green chilies. Simmer 30 minutes, stirring occasionally. Serves six hungry folks on January 6th, Epiphany Night.

Robert Hicks

SMOKY PORTOBELLO
MUSHROOM SOUP

¼ cup olive oil
Salt and pepper
½ cup chopped sweet onions
8 medium Portobello mushrooms
1½ Tbsp. chopped garlic
¼ cup white wine
24 oz. chicken stock
1 ¼ cup white roux (1 stick of butter and ½ cup all-purpose flour; cook slowly over low heat).
1 qt. heavy cream

Garnish - croutons, sour cream, and sliced chives

Preheat oven to 350 degrees.

Toss four of the Portobello mushrooms in oil and sprinkle with salt and pepper and roast them in the oven for approximately 45 minutes. Chop mushrooms into cubes.

In a large pot, sauté the onions in olive oil. Once onions are sautéed, add uncooked Portobello mushrooms and garlic. After mushrooms and garlic are cooked, add roasted mushrooms, white wine and chicken stock (or broth) and allow to simmer for 20 minutes.

Remove from heat and place mixture in blender. Add roux to pot. Blend in heavy cream. Place mixture back in pot on stove and add roux. Let simmer for 20 minutes.

Garnish with croutons, sour cream and sliced chives.

Lisa Parrish

TOMATO BISQUE

4 slices bacon
4 large garlic cloves, minced
6 celery stalks, chopped fine
2 onions, chopped fine
1 bay leaf
1 tsp. thyme
1 - 28 oz. can diced tomatoes with juice
1 - 8 oz. can tomato sauce
2 Tbsp. butter
3 Tbsp. flour
1 quart whipping cream at room temperature
1 small bay leaf
2 whole cloves
Salt and pepper to taste

Cook bacon, remove meat and save to put on top of soup. Add garlic to fat and sauté until lightly browned. Add celery, three-quarters of the chopped onions, bay leaf and thyme. Sauté until onions are transparent. Add tomatoes and tomato paste and bring to boil, stirring occasionally.

Reduce heat, cover and simmer for 30 minutes.

Start white sauce. Melt butter and stir in flour, bring to boil, stirring constantly. Remove from heat and slowly add cream, then add rest of the onion, bay leaf and cloves.

Cook over medium heat and cook uncovered for 45 minutes, stirring occasionally. Pour through fine strainer into tomato mixture and add salt and pepper to taste. Cover and simmer for about 15 minutes, stirring occasionally.

Soup can be topped with crumbled bacon and/or parmesan cheese if desired. I serve with cheese muffins.

Lynne Davis

LISA'S BEER CHEESE SOUP

6 - 8 slices of thick bacon, diced
6 oz. onion, diced
¼ cup butter
¼ cup all-purpose flour
2 ½ cups milk
16 oz. jar of Cheez Whiz
8 oz. chicken stock
1 tsp. Tabasco
2 - 3 Tbsp. Worcestershire sauce
¼ tsp. dry mustard
Salt and pepper to taste
1 can beer at room temperature

Fry bacon in skillet and drain on paper towels. In a large sauce pan, sauté onion in butter. Add flour and cook, stirring one minute. Add milk, Cheez Whiz, chicken stock, and spices. Cook stirring often on medium to low heat, until thickened. Add beer, and continue to stir. Let cook for 5 - 10 minutes, until beer is no longer fizzing.

Serve with home-made croutons.

CROUTONS

1 tsp. kosher salt
1 tsp. garlic powder
½ tsp. dried basil
¼ tsp. paprika
⅓ cup oil
4 cups bread cubes

Combine first four ingredients above and set aside until the croutons are done.

Heat oil in large non-stick skillet over medium-high heat. Add bread cubes and sauté until toasted, about 5 minutes, stirring often.

Toss croutons with seasonings while they are still warm.

Lisa Parrish

SOUPE AUX CHOUX

French cabbage soup has been a staple of Mary-Springs Scarborough-Couteaud's supper table at her farm in Normandy, France for many years. A former member of the board of directors at Carnton, Mary-Springs traded in life in the Bingham Community in Williamson County for her 17th Century farmhouse in the French countryside.

1 Tbsp. butter
2 Tbsp. extra virgin olive oil
½ lb. carrots, peeled, quartered length-wise, cut in 1 in. strips
½ lb. turnips, peeled and diced
½ lb. Irish potatoes, peeled and cubed
2 - 3 large leeks, well chopped
8 cups water
1 bay leaf
2 tsp. dried tarragon
2 tsp. kosher salt
½ tsp. ground pepper
1 cup Brussels sprouts
1 lb. Savoy cabbage
3 stalks celery

In an 8 quart saucepan, heat butter and olive oil. Add carrots, turnips, potatoes and leeks. Sauté for 5 to 10 minutes, stirring several times. Add water, bay leaf, tarragon, salt, pepper. Bring to boil.

Now simmer the soup over low heat for 40 minutes, covered. Stir several times. Remove bay leaf and add Brussels sprouts, Savoy cabbage and celery.

Cook for 15 minutes and serve six folks. You may add a cup of already boiled slivers of Tennessee or French country ham, both of which are cured with salt, before you brought the water to a boil. If you do, don't add the 2 teaspoons of salt.

Robert Hicks

LABOR IN VAIN
CORN CHOWDER

6 slices bacon
2 cups homemade chicken stock or 1 can of chicken broth
1 cup carrots, sliced
2 - 16 oz. cans whole corn, drained
½ tsp. ground pepper
3 cups milk
2 ½ cups potatoes, diced
1 cup onion, chopped
3 cups white cheddar cheese, shredded
3 Tbsp. flour

Fry up bacon, add onions, brown until bacon is crisp. Stir in chicken stock, carrots and potatoes. Simmer until the potatoes are tender, about 20 minutes, then stir in milk, corn and pepper. Bring to a simmer.

Mix in shredded cheese and flour. Stir until cheese is melted.

Robert Hicks

SAUSAGE SOUP

1 lb. sausage
1 medium onion, chopped
2 - 3 garlic cloves, minced
1 lb. mushrooms, sliced
1 tsp. pepper
Garlic powder to taste

1 bay leaf
1 tsp. basil
1 - 8 oz. can tomato sauce
1 large can chopped tomatoes
8 cups chicken broth
1 package rotini, cooked

Brown sausage without casing. Add garlic, onions, mushrooms, and remaining ingredients.

Bring to a boil. Simmer and serve.

Patti Caprara

CHEESY POTATO CHIVE SOUP

1 qt. mashed potatoes, seasoned with salt and pepper
2 tsp. freeze-dried chives
2 cups grated Velveeta cheese (not packed)
1 qt. milk or less for desired consistency

In double boiler heat milk and whisk in mashed potatoes. Add cheese and chives. Heat until hot; do not boil. Serve. You may add more chives if you'd like.

Marilyn Lehew

CARROT DILL BISQUE

2 qts. carrots, sliced or chopped
1 ⅓ qts. chicken stock
½ tsp. minced garlic
1 pt. heavy cream
1 medium onion, chopped
1 tsp. salt
½ tsp. white pepper
1/8 cup dry dill weed
2 tsp. sugar
¼ lb. butter, melted in small pot
⅔ cup flour

Combine carrots, onions, garlic, and chicken stock in large pot. Boil until carrots are tender. Puree in processor. Add remaining ingredients except butter and flour.

When soup is hot, mix flour and butter to form a roux; add to soup slowly, stirring constantly. Simmer 15 minutes.

Marilyn Lehew

VEGETARIAN CORN CHOWDER

1 qt. white sauce
3 cups frozen yellow corn, thawed
3 cups frozen white shoepeg corn, thawed
⅔ cup chopped fresh celery
⅓ cup chopped sweet onion
2 Tbsp. butter
Salt and pepper to taste.
1 tsp. sugar

Sauté celery and onion in butter. Grind ⅓ of each type of corn in food processor. Add corn to celery and onion mixture.

Heat slowly on low heat covered for 5 - 10 minutes. Add white sauce and heat slowly. Season to taste.

Marilyn Lehew

GAZPACHO

A favorite request from my family for special birthday dinners, along with homemade fried chicken and mashed potatoes. A tasty way to use all the delicious tomatoes from Carnton's garden.

3 tomatoes, diced
1 green pepper, diced
1 cucumber, peeled and diced
3 green onions, sliced
1 large jar V-8 juice

3 garlic cloves, minced
2 Tbsp. olive oil
2 Tbsp. red wine vinegar
Salt and pepper to taste

Combine all ingredients. Chill and serve.

May add a dollop of sour cream or baby shrimp.

Margie Thessin

PEACH SOUP

1 ½ lb. peaches, peeled and sliced
2 cups sour cream
1 cup orange juice
1 cup pineapple juice
½ cup dry sherry
1 Tbsp. lemon juice
Puree peaches in food processor. Add the rest of the ingredients and
sugar to taste. Chill.

Margaret Roberts

*Carrie McGavock, c.
1900, is wearing full
mourning attire. Carrie
survived John by 12 years,
passing away in 1905.*

Carnton's restored 1847 garden provides a bounty of heirloom fruit and vegetables each year. Much of the produce is picked by volunteers who then sell it and donate the proceeds to charity.

Salads

Camp Carnton is our week-long history camp for children ages 6-12. One year we instructed the children to pick their own snack from the Carnton garden. The youngsters hesitated at first, then after encouragement began to pick lettuce and carrots with gusto. They discovered to their utter shock that the carrots came up from the ground covered in dirt and required many washings. Unlike many of today's children, youngsters from the 19th century knew where their food came from.

Tomatoes, peppers, cucumbers, squash, potatoes, onions, grapes, carrots, lettuces, cabbages, even artichokes, were found in 19th century Middle Tennessee gardens. Today Carnton's garden replicates the location and plantings of the 1847 garden planted by Carrie McGavock. Many heirloom varieties found here today cannot be purchased commercially.

POTATO SALAD

Another recipe from the Tennessee Model Household Guide *by Carrie McGavock*

Boil your Irish potatoes carefully, cut in small slices with raw onions, and have a dressing of egg, raw or cooked, mustard, pepper, salt, and good vinegar, oil if desired, also a few cracker crumbs.

Carrie McGavock

CUKE-ONION SALAD

My mother Anne Rutherford suggested I send this cucumber salad recipe to you for the Carnton cookbook. This was a favorite recipe that came from her late sister, Lucinda Trabue Jamison. It is still a big favorite of our family and friends.

1 - 8 oz. pkg. cream cheese
1 cup mayonnaise
1 pkg. Knox gelatin
½ cup warm water
½ lemon
Dash Tabasco
Salt and pepper to taste
1 cup cucumber, chopped
½ cup onion, chopped

Mix together cream cheese and mayonnaise. Dissolve gelatin in water, mix with cream cheese and mayonnaise mixture, add lemon, Tabasco, salt and pepper. Add cucumber and onion. Refrigerate.

Lucinda Trabue Jamison, submitted by Becky Darby

GERMAN POTATO SALAD

8 medium potatoes
1 stalk celery, diced
1 medium onion, diced
2 hard-boiled eggs, sliced
4 slices bacon
2 raw eggs, well beaten

½ tsp. salt
½ tsp. pepper
¼ tsp. dry mustard
½ cup vinegar
½ cup water
½ cup sugar

Boil, peel and slice potatoes, add celery, onion and hard-boiled eggs. Fry bacon crisp, remove from grease and crumble over potatoes. Pour the beaten eggs, sugar, mustard, salt, pepper, vinegar and water in bacon grease. Cook slowly until it thickens slightly. Pour over potatoes. It is better to stand a few hours. May be reheated.

Nena Manci

SWEET BROCCOLI SLAW

2 - 12 oz. pkg. broccoli slaw mix
1 cup light or regular mayonnaise
½ cup sugar
2 Tbsp. cider vinegar
1 small red onion, chopped
½ cup sweetened dried cranberries
4 bacon slices, cooked and crumbled (You may omit this)

Stir together mayonnaise, sugar, and vinegar in a large bowl; add slaw, onion, and dried cranberries, tossing gently to mix.

Cover and chill a few hours before serving. Sprinkle with bacon before serving.

Nancy Moody

POTATO and GREEN BEAN SALAD

⅓ cup oil
3 Tbsp. cider vinegar
3 Tbsp. dried parsley flakes
1 bunch green onions, finely chopped
½ tsp. salt
5 medium potatoes, cooked and sliced
1 can sliced water chestnuts, drained and slightly chopped
1 can cut green beans, drained
Fresh ground pepper to taste

DRESSING

Combine oil, vinegar, parsley, onion, salt and pepper.

In a bowl layer warm potato slices and cover with dressing. Just before serving add green beans and water chestnuts. Toss lightly to mix.

Nena Manci

FROZEN LEMON SALAD

1 - 8 oz. pkg. cream cheese, softened
¼ cup sugar
¼ cup brown sugar
1 - 20 oz. can crushed pineapple, drained
2 cups lemon yogurt
1 tsp. ginger
2 Tbsp. pecans, chopped (optional)

Beat together cream cheese and both sugars until smooth. Add the rest of the ingredients. Put into aluminum foil muffin liners in muffin tins. Freeze. Peel off the foil liners before serving.

Margaret Roberts

MISSISSIPPI TOMATO ASPIC

This is delicious with chicken salad.

1 pkg. plain gelatin	Green olives
1 ⅔ cups V-8 juice	Bell pepper, chopped
Horseradish	Onion, grated
Lemon juice	Worcestershire sauce
Salt and pepper	

Soak gelatin in ⅔ cup of V-8 juice to soften. Heat remaining V-8 juice and add gelatin. Stir until dissolved.

Remove from heat and add to taste: horseradish, lemon juice, salt and pepper, green olives, bell pepper, onion and Worcestershire sauce

Pour into Jell-O molds and refrigerate overnight.

Margaret Roberts

CHITUNA SALAD

1 - 6 oz. can tuna, drained
1 - 6 oz. can chicken, drained
2 oz. cheddar cheese, shredded
2 Tbsp. pickle relish
2 scallions, chopped finely

1 tsp. stone ground Dijon
mustard
2 - 3 Tbsp. mayonnaise
Garlic powder, seasoning salt,
dill and black pepper to taste

Mix all ingredients. Serve on a bed of lettuce, on a whole quartered
tomato or make sandwiches.

Nena Manci

CAESAR SALAD

SALAD

Romaine lettuce
Croutons
Parmesan cheese

DRESSING

2 garlic cloves, peeled
2 Tbsp. fresh lemon juice
1 large egg or 1 Tbsp.
mayonnaise
1 tsp. Worcestershire sauce

½ tsp. salt
½ cup extra virgin olive oil
3 or 4 anchovy fillets, mashed to
a paste
Salt and pepper to taste

Mash garlic cloves, anchovies and salt together in a small bowl until a
paste is formed. Whisk in the lemon juice, egg or mayonnaise and
Worcestershire sauce. Add olive oil in a slow, steady stream, whisking
constantly.

Toss salad with dressing before serving. Top with grated or sliced
shaved Parmesan (I slice or shave it) and mix it in with the greens before
the dressing.

Vicki Stout

CRUNCHY TUNA SALAD

1 can tuna (you can substitute chicken)
1 cup shredded carrots
¾ cup celery, chopped
¼ cup onion, minced
¾ cup mayonnaise
1 - 7 oz. can shoestring potato sticks

Combine all ingredients except potato sticks, and chill. When ready to serve, stir in potato sticks and serve on lettuce.

Ona B. Faulkner

SPINACH SALAD

This recipe was provided by Mary Carr, the wife of Winder Heller, a direct descendant of Carrie and John McGavock through their son Winder.

SALAD

8 oz. baby spinach leaves
½ cup bleu cheese, crumbled
Walnut halves or pistachio nuts
½ cup dried cranberries

Sauté walnut halves in olive oil with brown sugar sprinkled on (or use roasted pistachio nuts). Toss all ingredients in salad bowl.

DRESSING

½ tsp. sugar
Salt and pepper to taste
⅓ cup olive oil
⅙ cup balsamic vinegar

Make dressing in a jar, then pour over salad and toss.

Mary Carr

SWEET SOUR SPINACH SALAD

SALAD

1 bag spinach
1 can sliced water chestnuts, drained
2 hard-cooked eggs, chopped
5 strips bacon, fried and crumbled
1 small can bean sprouts, drained
Mushrooms, sliced

DRESSING

¾ cup sugar
1 cup salad oil
1 small onion
3 Tbsp. Worcestershire sauce
⅓ cup ketchup
¼ cup vinegar
¼ tsp. salt

Mix in blender and put dressing on salad 15 minutes before serving.

Ellen DiLorenzo

PEAR AND APPLE SALAD

1 Bosc pear, chunked
1 Granny Smith apple, chunked
¼ cup cashew halves
¼ cup dried cranberries or
Craisins

¼ cup Asiago cheese, shredded
6 cups romaine lettuce, torn
Jar poppy seed dressing

Toss in bowl with bottled poppy seed dressing—just enough to cover lettuce.

Patti Caprara

Strawberry salads are so popular these days. Here are three of the best!

PATTI'S STRAWBERRY SPRING SALAD

SALAD

Boston, bibb or leaf lettuce
mixture
½ qt. strawberries, sliced

½ lb. feta cheese, crumbled
(more or less to taste)
½ cup sliced almonds, toasted

DRESSING

½ cup plus 2 tsp. red wine
vinegar
½ cup sugar
½ cup oil

½ tsp. dry mustard
2 cloves fresh garlic, chopped
½ tsp. paprika

Heat sugar and vinegar until dissolved. Add remaining ingredients and
chill. Just before serving add dressing to taste and toss.

Patti Caprara

CANDIE'S STRAWBERRY SALAD

FIRST LAYER

2 cups crushed pretzels (not too
fine)

½ cup sugar
½ cup margarine, melted

Mix together and pat into a 9 x 13 inch pan. Bake at 350 degrees for 8
minutes. Cool before adding 2nd layer.

SECOND LAYER

1 - 8 oz. pkg. cream cheese, softened
1 cup sugar
1 - 8 oz. tub Cool Whip

Mix together and spread on top of cooled pretzel crust.

THIRD LAYER

1 - 6 oz. pkg. strawberry Jell-O
2 cups boiling water
2 - 16 oz. pkg. frozen strawberries, partially thawed

Mix Jell-O and water together and let stand for about 10 minutes. Then add the partially thawed strawberries and pour over the second layer. Refrigerate until firm.

Candie Westbrook

BONNIE'S STRAWBERRY SALAD

SALAD

Spring mix (whatever amount you need, you can add chopped romaine to stretch)
1 cup Monterey Jack cheese, shredded

½ cup toasted pecans or walnuts
1 pint sliced strawberries
1 can mandarin oranges (optional)

DRESSING

1 cup oil (I use half olive & half canola)
½ cup red wine vinegar
½ tsp. salt

¼ tsp. ground white pepper
¾ cup sugar (I use Splenda)
1 tsp. garlic, minced
½ tsp. paprika

Mix above ingredients in a jar or bottle and shake well. If you put the dressing in a squeeze or pour bottle, be sure the tip is large enough so the garlic will not clog the pouring spout.

Pour dressing on salad just before serving.

Bonnie Ingle

OLIVE-CORN MEXICALI SALAD

1 - 6 oz. can black olives chopped and drained
1 - 16 oz. can whole corn, drained
1 - 3 to 4 oz. can cocktail onions drained
¼ cup green pepper, diced
2 Tbsp. oil
¼ cup lemon juice
¼ cup lime juice
½ tsp. sugar
1 tsp. salt
½ tsp. Tabasco
1 cup thin tomato wedges
⅓ cup parsley, finely diced

Mix everything together and refrigerate for at least 4 hours. Serve.

Martha Thuma

HENNY PENNY PASTA SALAD

1 - 8 oz. package rotini or shell pasta
1 bunch broccoli (about 1 ½ pounds)
4 chicken breast halves, cooked and skinned
½ cup chopped sweet red or yellow pepper
¼ cup ripe olives, sliced
1 Tbsp. green onion, sliced
½ cup sour cream
¼ cup mayonnaise
3 Tbsp. white wine vinegar
2 Tbsp. heavy cream
1 tsp. salt
1 tsp. dried tarragon, crushed
¼ tsp. cayenne pepper
½ tsp. curry powder

Cook rotini or shells according to package directions. Rinse under cold water; drain. Cut broccoli into flowerets; cook in a small amount of boiling water for 3 to 5 minutes or until crisp-tender. Drain. Remove chicken from bones; cut into bit-size pieces. In a large bowl, combine pasta, broccoli, chicken, red pepper, ripe olives, and green onion. Toss lightly. In a small bowl, stir together sour cream, mayonnaise, wine vinegar, cream, salt, tarragon, curry powder and pepper. Pour over pasta mixture and toss. Cover and chill.

Lisa Patton

OLD FASHIONED MACARONI SALAD

1 lb. cooked elbow macaroni
½ cup chopped celery
½ carrot, grated
6 chopped scallions
8 to 12 sliced pimento-stuffed
olives

½ to ¾ cup mayonnaise
1 tsp. sugar
1 Tbsp. celery seed
Salt and pepper to taste

Drain the pasta, but do not rinse. Cool slightly. Mix in all ingredients.
Best eaten at room temperature the day it is made.

Marilyn Lehew

*Windermere was built for Carrie McGavock's mother Martha Grundy Winder after
she was widowed in 1854. The house was recently purchased by descendants after
many years. Windermere's property adjoins Carnton's.*

Carnton's smokehouse is original to the site and predates the historic house. It was one of the first structures on the property, c. 1815.

Main Courses

With large quantities of pork, beef, lamb and chicken as well as game available, main courses centered around meats in the 19th century. The large smokehouse at Carnton was used to cure and smoke a variety of meat products. These kinds of smoked and salted meats were a part of the typical 19th century diet. Pictured at left is the original Carnton smokehouse, built c. 1815. The inside walls are still black from the smoke.

CHICKEN CROQUETTES

Another recipe from the Tennessee Model Household Guide, *attributed to Mrs. C.W. McG. from Franklin, Tenn.*

Boil your fowl well, chop as fine as possible, add salt, pepper, a little mace, ginger, and mustard, or a little chowchow* pickle well drained. Add 4 beaten eggs, a little flour, and bread crumbs. Stew all together a few minutes, and when cool make into cone-shaped balls, roll in pulverized cracker crumbs, and fry in hot lard. For the fowl you can substitute any cold meat.

Carrie Winder McGavock

*For Carrie's chowchow pickle recipe, see p. 93.

Poultry

CHICKEN LOAF

2 boiled hens, cut in large pieces
2 cups cream sauce
1 cup bread crumbs
4 eggs

1 pt. cream
2 lbs. mushrooms
¼ lb. butter
1 cup thickened stock

Put in two buttered bread pans and bake 1 hour in 325 degree oven. Make sauce of cream broiled mushrooms, butter and stock.

Louise Reid McGavock

SMOKED TURKEY WRAPS

Great for Carnton picnics!

2 - 6 ½ oz. pkgs. garlic and herb flavored cheese, softened
8 - 10 inch pita wraps or tortillas
Caramelized onions (see below)
1 ½ lb. thinly sliced smoked turkey

16 bacon slices, cooked and crumbled
4 cups loosely packed mixed baby salad greens

Spread cheese evenly over pitas or tortillas; top evenly with caramelized onions and remaining ingredients. Roll up, and wrap in parchment paper; chill. Cut in half to serve. 8 servings

CARAMELIZED ONIONS

2 large sweet onions, diced
1 Tbsp. sugar

2 Tbsp. olive oil
2 tsp. balsamic vinegar

Cook onion and sugar in hot oil over medium high heat, stirring often, until onion is caramel colored. Stir in vinegar. This can be done ahead.

Nancy Moody

CHICKEN CACCIATORE

5 chicken breasts
2 cloves garlic, minced
1 medium onion, diced
3 - 15 oz. cans of tomato sauce
2 - 1 lb. cans of chopped tomatoes
1½ tsp. salt
2 tsp. oregano
1 tsp. celery seed
¼ tsp. pepper
2 bay leaves

Slowly brown chicken in oil. Once cooked, cut into small pieces, remove from pan. Brown the garlic and onion in oil. Mix all remaining ingredients into a sauce. Add chicken, onion, and garlic to sauce. Cover and simmer 45 minutes. Uncover and cook for 20 more minutes. Remove bay leaves and serve over rice or thin spaghetti.

Patti Caprara

LEMON BASIL GRILLED CHICKEN

½ cup olive oil
¼ cup lemon juice
2 Tbsp. white wine vinegar
1 tsp. grated lemon peel
1 Tbsp. dried basil

2 cloves garlic, minced
½ tsp. salt
¼ tsp. fresh ground pepper
4 boneless, skinless chicken breast halves (about 1 lb.)

Combine oil and next 7 ingredients in shallow baking dish or substitute gallon zip-lock bag. Add chicken, turning once to coat both sides. Refrigerate for 30 - 45 minutes, turning once. Prepare charcoal for grilling, or heat broiler.

Grill or broil chicken 4 inches from heat, turning once, 3 - 5 minutes per side or until completely cooked through.

Nena Manci

COMPANY CHICKEN

6 boneless, skinless chicken breasts
Dash of salt, pepper, and paprika
½ cup butter or margarine
¼ tsp. sweet basil
¼ tsp. rosemary

½ cup onion, chopped
1 - 4 oz. can sliced mushrooms, drained
¼ cup cooking sherry
Juice of ½ lemon
1 can cream of mushroom soup
3 cups hot cooked rice

Place chicken in a greased shallow baking dish. Sprinkle with salt, pepper, and paprika.

Melt butter or margarine in large sauce pan. Add remaining ingredients, except rice. Stir until blended; pour over chicken. Bake at 350 degrees for 1 hour and 15 minutes.

When ready to serve, remove chicken from baking dish. Mix gravy and rice together and place chicken breasts on mound of rice to serve.

Lucy Battle

BAKED MUSTARD CHICKEN

4 chicken breast halves, skinned
¼ cup spicy brown mustard
½ cup Italian-flavored bread crumbs

¼ cup butter, melted
2 Tbsp. lemon juice
2 Tbsp. white wine or water
Paprika

Brush chicken with mustard and dredge in breadcrumbs. Place in a 13 x 9 x 2 inch baking dish. Combine butter, lemon juice and wine; drizzle 1 tablespoon over each piece of chicken, and pour remainder in dish.

Cover and bake at 350 degrees for 45 minutes. Remove cover, sprinkle with paprika and bake an additional 15 minutes.

Mary Jo Kiker

SWEET and SOUR CHICKEN

6 boneless chicken breasts
3 Tbsp. oil
1 medium onion, cut in thin
strips
1 medium green pepper, cut in
thin strips
1 medium red pepper, cut in
thin strips
1 garlic clove, minced

¾ cup ketchup
½ cup water
¾ cup sugar
⅓ cup lemon juice
4 Tbsp. Worcestershire sauce
2 Tbsp. prepared mustard
Salt and pepper to taste
Pineapple tidbits to taste

Place chicken in baking dish. Heat oil and saute onion, peppers and garlic until soft. Combine rest of ingredients. Pour into pepper mixture and bring to a boil. Pour over chicken and bake at 350 degrees uncovered for 45 -50 minutes or till done, depending on size of the chicken breasts. Stir in pineapple tidbits to taste the last 5 minutes of cooking. Serve over rice. 6 servings

Nancy Moody

CHICKEN CASUELA

6 chicken breasts with skin and
bone in
2 cloves garlic, chopped
⅔ stick butter
Flour
Salt

Pepper
Paprika to taste
1 - 4 oz. jar stuffed green olives
1 cup white wine or sherry
1 - 4 oz. can mushrooms,
drained and sliced

Salt, pepper, flour and paprika the chicken breasts lightly. In skillet melt butter and add garlic and chicken. Brown quickly then remove from skillet. Put mushrooms and sliced olives in skillet in which chicken was browned. Add wine, stir well. Put chicken breasts back in skillet and baste well with the wine butter mixture.

Cook one hour in a 325 degree oven. Good served over rice.

GRILLED MARINATED
CORNISH GAME HENS

½ cup olive oil
½ cup orange juice
2 Tbsp. soy sauce
½ cup wine vinegar
2 dashes red pepper sauce
¼ tsp. Worcestershire sauce
¼ tsp. dried thyme leaves
¼ tsp. coarse black pepper
½ tsp. salt
2 Cornish game hens, split (see note*)

Combine all ingredients, except game hens.

Place hens in glass dish and cover with marinade or substitute gallon zipper bag. Marinate 4 - 5 hours turning occasionally.

Grill over low coals, basting with marinade until well done, about 1 hour.

* Note: To split hens, remove giblets package and place hens, breast side down and legs facing you, On a cutting board, using a very sharp knife, cut through the piece of cartilage at the end of the breast facing you.

Remember, the breast side of the hen is on the cutting board. Turn hens over so that breast is up, finish cutting breast in half. Then place knife on inside of back, pressing the sharp edge through the backbone.

This recipe is good as marinade using boneless, skinless chicken breast halves. Cook about 3 - 5 minutes each side until completely cooked through.

Nena Manci

CHICKEN ALMONDZINI

¾ cup mayonnaise
½ cup flour
2 Tbsp. minced onion
1 tsp. garlic salt
2 ¼ cups milk
1 cup shredded Swiss cheese
⅓ cup dry white wine

3 cups chopped cooked chicken
7 oz. spaghetti cooked
1-10 oz. pkg. frozen chopped broccoli, thawed and drained
1 ¼ cups sliced almonds
1 - 4 oz. can sliced mushrooms
¼ cup diced pimento (optional)

In medium saucepan combine mayonnaise, flour and seasonings. Gradually add milk, cook over low heat stirring constantly until thickened. Add cheese and wine.

Stir until cheese melts. In large bowl combine mayonnaise mixture, spaghetti, chicken, broccoli, ¾ cup of almonds, mushrooms and pimento. Toss lightly.

Pour mixture into 11 x 7 ½ baking dish. Top with remaining almonds. Bake at 350 degrees 40 - 45 minutes until thoroughly heated. Serve with grated parmesan cheese. If you double the recipe, don't double the sauce - just half it again and double the other ingredients.

Anne Rutherford

CHICKEN ROLLUPS

2 chicken breasts
Olive oil spray
Feta cheese

Fresh spinach, uncooked
Mrs. Dash
Fresh ground black pepper

Pound chicken breast thin. Spray with oil olive and sprinkle pepper and Mrs. Dash. Place cheese and spinach on chicken breast. Roll up and affix with a toothpick. Spray top with olive oil spray and bake at 350 degrees for 20-30 minutes.

Becky Short

CHICKEN PARISIENNE (CROCK POT STYLE)

This recipe can be made ahead and easily doubled, tripled and even quadrupled.

6 chicken breasts, boned
½ cup white wine
1 - 10 oz. can cream of
mushroom soup
½ cup mushrooms, sliced

1 cup sour cream
¼ cup flour
Salt
Pepper
Paprika

COOKING DAY

Mix wine, soup and mushrooms together. Stir flour into sour cream and add to soup mixture. At this point, place mixture together with chicken in a freezer bag.

SERVING DAY

Place chicken and sauce in a crock pot. Sprinkle salt, pepper and paprika over top. Cover and cook on low for 6 - 8 hrs.

Nena Manci

This portrait of three of the McGavock children hangs in the master bedroom. From left, they are Mary Elizabeth, Martha and John Randal.

TUSCAN CHICKEN CAKES
with TOMATO-BASIC RELISH

3 cups cooked chicken, shredded
⅓ cup balsamic dressing
1 cup Italian bread crumbs, divided
1 cup mayonnaise
1 egg, lightly beaten
¼ cup basil pesto
2 tsp. honey mustard
⅓ cup roasted red peppers, chopped and drained
⅓ cup chopped red onion
2 tsp. olive oil
1 - 5 oz. pkg. salad greens
⅓ cup golden aioli (½ cup mayonnaise and 2 Tbsp. honey mustard)

In large mixing bowl, mix chicken, egg, half of bread crumbs, mayonnaise, pesto, honey mustard, peppers and onion. Use a ⅓ cup measuring cup to form into cakes.

Dip each cake into the additional bread crumbs and brown in oil, about 3 minutes per side. Toss greens with dressing and serve cakes over greens.

Drizzle cakes with golden aioli and top with a dollop of tomato basil relish.

TOMATO BASIL RELISH

1 cup fresh tomato
⅓ cup red onion,
3 Tbsp. sun dried tomatoes, chopped and drained

2 Tbsp. fresh basil
2 Tbsp balsamic dressing
1 tsp. pesto

Mix all ingredients together.

Ginny Holley

Pork

PULLED PORK

3 Tbsp. brown sugar	1 ½ tsp. salt
3 Tbsp. paprika	½ cup Dijon mustard
1 ½ Tbsp. garlic powder	8 - 9 lbs. bone-in pork shoulder
1 ½ Tbsp. ground black pepper	butt roast, rind removed

Adjust oven rack to lowest position and heat oven to 250 degrees. In a small bowl, mix sugar, paprika, garlic powder, pepper and salt to make a dry rub. Line a shallow pan with foil. Pat the pork dry. Place it on a rack set over the pan. Lightly sprinkle the top and sides of the meat with additional salt, brush with half the mustard, then sprinkle with half the dry rub. Carefully turn roast over. Repeat process with a little extra salt and the remaining mustard and dry rub.

Place pork in oven and roast until a meat thermometer registers 170 degrees (9 - 11 hours). Remove pork from oven. Let sit until cool enough to handle, about 1 hour. Meanwhile, scrape pan drippings into a small saucepan, add 1 cup water and barbecue sauce.

Marilyn Lehew

KIRK'S SPARE RIBS

Spare ribs in quantity desired
Cavender's Greek Seasoning
Barbeque sauce

Rub ribs all over with Cavender's. Heat oven to 220 degrees. Place in rib rack, cook approximately 7 hours.

Then place on charcoal grill, slather with your favorite barbecue sauce, cook another 30 minutes.

Kirk Lucas

STUFFED PORK CHOPS

6 pork chops, 1 in. thick
4 Tbsp. shortening
6 Tbsp. onion, chopped
1 Tbsp. green pepper, chopped
2 Tbsp. celery, chopped
1 tsp. salt
2 cups bread crumbs
½ cup Pet milk
½ cup cracker meal

Split the chops through the center to the bone, making a pocket to hold the stuffing. Melt half the shortening and in it cook the onion until delicately browned.

Add chopped pepper, celery, salt and bread crumbs. Moisten with milk, fill chops with stuffing and fasten with small wooden skewers. Dip in undiluted Pet milk and again in meal. Brown in remaining shortening.

Sprinkle with salt and pepper and add enough water to cover bottom of pan. Bake at 350 degrees until tender, about one hour.

Hattie McGavock Ayres

PORK CHOPS A LA BABETTE

6 pork chops
½ cup flour
¼ tsp. dry mustard
Salt and pepper to taste
1 can chicken and rice soup

Combine flour, mustard, salt and pepper. Dredge pork chops in flour mixture. Place in crock pot. Pour soup over pork chops and cook on low for 6 - 8 hours.

Babette Mackey

HERBED PORK ROAST

4 - 6 lb. loin of pork
2 ½ tsp. salt
1 tsp. pepper
1 tsp. thyme
½ tsp. nutmeg
2 carrots, cut up
2 onions, coarsely chopped

2 garlic cloves, minced
4 whole cloves
Few chopped celery leaves
Few springs of parsley
3 bay leaves
1 can chicken broth

Combine salt, pepper, thyme and nutmeg; rub into meat. Bake uncovered at 450 degrees for 30 minutes. Reduce temperature to 350 degrees and add remaining ingredients. Cover and bake about three hours or until meat is tender, basting often. Before serving, remove roast to warm platter. Blend pan juices and vegetables in blender to serve as gravy. Skim fat, if necessary. May be prepared a day ahead of time and be reheated.

Lucy Battle

ROAST PORK TENDERLOIN

This was my mother Barbara Hillebrand's recipe.

2 or 3 (individual) pork
tenderloins approximately 1 ½
lbs. each
½ cup real maple syrup
½ cup ketchup
¾ cup water

½ tsp. salt
½ tsp. celery salt
1½ Tbsp. flour
Crisco
Margarine

Mix maple syrup, ketchup, ¼ cup water, salt and celery salt together. Dust tenderloin with flour, salt and pepper to taste. Brown slowly in small amount of margarine and Crisco. Mix the other ingredients for sauce. Pour over browned meat in covered pan and then cover and bake at 350 degrees for 1 ½ hours. Remove to platter and add the flour shaken with ½ cup water to sauce and thicken. Pour onto tenderloin after slicing in serving dish.

Carole Guthrie

MARINATED PORK TENDERLOIN

½ cup oil
2 Tbsp. molasses
1 Tbsp. ground ginger
2 tsp. dry mustard
6 cloves garlic, minced
½ cup soy sauce (I use low sodium)

Marinate overnight. Cook 2 hours at 325 degrees. Serve over rice. Add roasted asparagus and cornbread and you have one of our favorite meals!

Lynne Davis

Carnton, shown here from the front, as it appeared sometime in the mid- to late- 19th century. This is probably the earliest photograph of Carnton.

CHILI RELLENO BAKE

1 lb. ground chuck
1 lb. ground sausage
2 cloves garlic, minced
1 cup salsa
1 can Mexican Rotel tomatoes
1 roasted Poblano pepper, diced
10 - 12 corn tortillas, cut into strips
2 cups shredded Monterey Jack cheese
2 cups sharp cheddar cheese, shredded
⅓ cup yellow cornmeal
4 large eggs
¼ cup all-purpose flour
1½ cups milk
½ tsp. salt
¼ tsp. hot sauce
Garnish: sour cream, chopped fresh cilantro

Preheat oven to 350 degrees. Lightly grease a 13 x 9 inch baking dish.

In a large skillet, combine ground chuck, ground sausage, onion, and garlic. Cook over medium heat, stirring occasionally, until meat is browned and crumbly. Drain well. Stir in salsa and Rotel tomatoes.

After roasting pepper, remove seeds and dice. Place half of corn tortillas in bottom of baking dish. Spoon half of meat mixture over tortillas. Sprinkle diced peppers over the meat mixture, then sprinkle evenly with half of cheese.

Place remaining tortillas in an even layer over cheese. Spoon remaining meat mixture over tortillas. Top evenly with remaining cheese. Sprinkle cornmeal evenly over cheese.

In a medium bowl, whisk together eggs and flour until smooth. Whisk in milk, salt, and hot sauce. Pour over cornmeal. Bake 35 - 45 minutes or until set. Let cool 10 minutes. Cut into squares to serve. Garnish with sour cream and chopped fresh cilantro, if desired.

Lisa Parrish

SWISS STEAK

Hattie was a popular name in the McGavock family. John and Carrie had a daughter named Hattie. This Hattie was John and Carrie's granddaughter through their son Winder.

3 lbs. round steak
1 Tbsp. flour
1 tsp. salt
½ tsp. pepper
2 onions, minced
1 lemon, juiced
2 sweet peppers, sliced
2 cups water
½ bottle ketchup

Pound in flour, salt and pepper. Sear on both sides, add onions, lemon, peppers. Add water and ketchup. Reduce heat and cook slowly for two hours.

Hattie McGavock Ayres

SCOTCH STEW

This was our traditional Sunday night meal, served over homemade waffles! I know that it sounds terrible but it really was delicious. It could also be served over potatoes or rice.

1 lb. ground round   Pepper
Water   2 Tbsp. butter
Salt   Onion, chopped (optional)

Cover meat with water. Let cook slowly until water is cooked down very low. Add butter and onion, if desired.

Elizabeth McGavock Darby and daughter Mary Margaret Cain

MOLLY'S MEATLOAF
with ROASTED POTATOES

1 lb. ground beef
1 egg
2 slices bread, shredded
½ cup ketchup
½ cup grated cheddar cheese

1 medium red onion, diced
½ tsp. salt
½ tsp. pepper
Olive oil
Garlic salt

Mix beef, egg, bread, ketchup, cheese, onion, salt and pepper together in large bowl. Place in foil-lined 9 x 13 inch glass pan and mold in loaf shape. Peel potatoes, cut in chunks and place around meatloaf. Brush with olive oil, sprinkle with garlic salt and pepper.
Bake one hour at 350 degrees.

Molly Thessin

BEEF and BROCCOLI PIE

This is a great one-dish meal that my kids loved growing up. Just serve with a nice salad.

1 lb. ground beef
¼ cup chopped onion
2 Tbsp. flour
¾ tsp. salt
¼ tsp. garlic
1 ¼ cup milk

1 - 3 oz. pkg. cream cheese, softened
1 egg, beaten
1 - 10 oz. pkg. frozen chopped, cooked broccoli, drained
2 pkgs. crescent rolls
4 oz. Monterey Jack cheese

In a skillet, cook beef and onion; drain. Stir in flour, salt and garlic. Add milk and cream cheese. Cook and stir until thick and smooth. Add a little to the beaten egg and return to skillet. Cook for 1 - 2 minutes. Stir in broccoli. Place the crescent rolls in pie plate. Fill shell with mixture. Cut cheese in slices and place on top of mixture. Cover with more rolls. Brush with milk. Bake at 350 degrees for 30 minutes.

Martha Thuma

FLANK STEAK

1 flank steak
¼ cup soy sauce
2 Tbsp. vinegar
2 Tbsp. onion flakes

Garlic powder to equal 1 clove garlic
1½ tsp. ginger
Artificial sweetener to equal ½ cups sugar

Combine soy sauce, vinegar, onion flakes, garlic powder, ginger and artificial sweetener in container large enough to hold flank steak. Place flank steak in mixture and let marinate overnight in refrigerator.

Grill steak to desired temperature.

Carole Guthrie

DRIED BEEF IN SOUR CREAM

This was always a special breakfast treat for my family, sometimes on a holiday morning.

¼ lb. dried beef
¼ cup butter
2 Tbsp. minced onion
1 cup milk
1 cup sour cream
1 can sliced mushrooms
(or 1 cup fresh sliced mushrooms)

1 cup sharp cheese, shredded
2 Tbsp. parsley, chopped
3 Tbsp. flour
Salt and pepper to taste
English muffins, toasted

Cut the beef in strips. In a large saucepan melt the butter. Add onion and cook three minutes. Blend in flour. Add milk. Cook, stirring well until thickened. Add sour cream, mushrooms, cheese, parsley, salt & pepper. Stir well; heat through. Serve over toasted English muffins.

Martha Thuma

Seafood

SARAH OWEN EWING'S SCALLOPED OYSTERS

This recipe came from a descendant of the James and Louisa McGavock family who lived in Franklin at a house called Riverside, which is in today's Forrest Crossing subdivision. Their daughter Sarah married Randal Milton Ewing.

1 pt. standard oysters (after picking through for shell bits)
¾ stick butter
2 cups whole milk

Cracker crumbs, medium to large
Red (Cayenne) pepper
Black pepper

Simmer oysters, pepper and butter in pan until curled. Pour in milk and heat. Add cracker crumbs to a somewhat mushy consistency. Put in casserole. Butter the top. Cook in 450 degree oven.

Sarah Ewing Parker Peay

CAJUN CATFISH with PECAN CRUST

¼ cup fine dry bread crumbs
2 tsp. Cajun seafood seasoning
4 catfish fillets, about 6 oz. each

¼ cup pecan pieces, chopped
1 Tbsp. butter, melted
Juice of 1 lemon

Preheat oven to 450 degrees. Spray a 9 x 13 inch baking dish with cooking spray.

Mix the bread crumbs and Cajun seasoning on waxed paper to combine. Coat the fillets with the crumb mixture and place skin side down in the baking dish. Sprinkle the top of the fish with the finely chopped pecans. Squeeze the lemon juice over the fish. Spoon the melted butter evenly over the fillets. Bake, uncovered, until the fish is opaque throughout and flakes easily with a fork, 12 - 14 minutes.

Nancy Moody

LISA'S CRAB CAKES

1 lb. crab meat
¼ cup shredded parmesan cheese
2 Tbsp. melted butter
2 Tbsp. sour cream
2 eggs, beaten
1 Tbsp. Worcestershire sauce
4 or 5 drops hot sauce

2 green onions, chopped
2 Tbsp. fresh parsley, chopped
Juice from 1 lemon
1 tsp. dry mustard
Salt and freshly ground pepper
1 cup Italian seasoned bread crumbs

Mix all ingredients together with a wire whisk, except for crab meat and bread crumbs. Add crab and bread crumbs and gently mix together. Form crab cakes and refrigerate for at least 1 hour before cooking. Cook in a medium hot skillet in 2 tablespoons butter for oil. Cook until brown, about 4 minutes per side.

Serve with remoulade sauce. I use Louisiana Fish Fry remoulade sauce.

Lisa Parrish

BBQ SHRIMP

Be sure to have French bread ready to soak up the wonderful sauce.

50 Shrimp
1 stick butter
1 large bottle Italian dressing
1 ½ onions

Garlic
1 bottle Pickapepper sauce
Worcestershire sauce

After melting butter, add onion, Italian dressing, Pickapepper sauce, and Worcestershire sauce (to taste). Marinate shrimp for 30 minutes.

Bake at 450 degrees for 35 minutes.

To test, raise a shrimp to the light. If shrimp has come away from its shell, it's ready.

Kristin Duke

Harry Kenning, looking dapper, is 2nd from right in the photo above. From left to right are Winder McGavock, Leah Cowan, Hattie McGavock Cowan, A. B. Ewing, Kenning and George Cowan.

SEAFOOD GUMBO

Harry Kenning was an orphan taken in by Carrie and John McGavock in the late 19th century. Harry remained faithful to the McGavocks, acting as a pallbearer at Carrie's funeral in 1905. He named his daughter Hattie and his son Winder after John and Carrie's children. He is in the c. 1906 photo at left, along with McGavock family members.

Joan Young, a long-time Carnton board member and supporter, is his granddaughter.

1 cup salad or olive oil
1 cup flour
2 large onions, chopped
1 cup celery, chopped
1 large green pepper
6 cloves garlic, chopped fine
1 - 1 lb. can tomatoes
1 qt. water
2 qts. chicken broth
½ cup chopped parsley

½ cup green onions, chopped
¼ tsp. thyme
2 Tbsp. salt
½ tsp. pepper
4 cups okra, sliced
¼ lb. ham
1 lb. shrimp
1 lb. crabmeat
1 pt. oysters

Combine oil and flour in a heavy skillet over medium heat. Cook, stirring constantly until the roux is the color of a copper penny. Add onion, celery, green pepper and garlic to the roux.

Cook stirring constantly until the vegetables are tender. Gradually add liquids to the roux, blending well. Add okra and tomatoes. Simmer for 20 minutes.

Add salt, pepper, ham and seafood, bring to a boil and simmer for 10 minutes. Add parsley and green onion and simmer 5 minutes. Serve over hot rice.

Chicken can be added or substituted for seafood.

Joan Young

OYSTER SPAGHETTI

6 oz. sharp cheddar cheese, grated
1 large onion, chopped
3 - 4 stalks celery, chopped
1 large bunch green onions, chopped
½ cup all-purpose flour
½ cup olive oil
½ lb. chicken livers
1 can evaporated skim milk
1 lb. thin spaghetti
1 qt. oysters
Saltines
Parmesan cheese
Margarine
Salt, red and black pepper to taste, or Tony Chachere's Seasoning

Preheat oven to 350 degrees. Spray a large casserole dish with cooking spray. Boil spaghetti and remove from heat and drain at al dente stage. Cover chicken livers in small saucepan with 2 or 3 cups water. Toss in ends from the onion and celery. Bring to a boil and simmer gently while making roux.

For roux, combine flour and olive oil in Dutch oven, over low heat, stirring often. Meanwhile, chop onion, celery and green onions. Increase the heat under the Dutch oven to medium and stir roux until it is dark caramel in color. Add the chopped seasoning and stir well. Remove the chicken livers from the heat. Remove livers from saucepan, reserving liquid and chop into gumdrop size pieces.

Drain oysters well. Add chopped livers to roux and reduce heat to low. Strain liquid from the chicken livers into the roux, mixing well. Add salt and peppers to taste. Add drained oysters; stir well. Add evaporated skim milk (shaken). Mix thoroughly. Spoon half the spaghetti mixture into the casserole dish.

Sprinkle with half the grated cheese. Spoon on remaining spaghetti mixture. Top with remaining cheddar cheese. Sprinkle with cracker crumbs and Parmesan cheese and dot with margarine. Bake 45 - 50 minutes or until lightly browned and bubbly. Can be made ahead, refrigerated, then warmed slowly.

Becky Barkley

SHRIMP JAMBALAYA

My very favorite dish for company.

1 cup onion, diced	1 ½ tsp. salt
1 clove garlic, minced	Dash cayenne, cloves and
¾ cup green peppers, diced	nutmeg
1 cup cooked ham, diced	¼ cup parsley, chopped
1 cup butter	3 ½ cans tomatoes
2 chicken bouillon cubes	2 cups oysters and liquid
1 ½ cups boiling water	1 ½ lbs. raw shrimp
½ tsp. thyme	1 cup uncooked rice

Sauté onions, garlic, green pepper and ham in butter in deep pan. Cook until vegetables are just tender. Combine bouillon and water and add to pan plus seasoning, parsley and tomatoes.

About 45 minutes before serving, bring to a boil and add rice. When rice is nearly done, dump in oysters and shrimp and cook about 10 minutes. Don't overcook.

Anne Rutherford

GINGER-SOY MARINADE

Great for halibut, salmon, swordfish and tuna.

1 tsp. garlic, crushed
2 Tbsp. soy sauce
2 tsp. sherry
2 Tbsp. vegetable oil
1 Tbsp. sugar
1 Tbsp. ginger, minced

Mix. Store. Marinate fish 2 hours. Bake, broil or grill fish until done.

Marilyn Lehew

STUFFED SHRIMP

MARINADE

¼ cup olive oil
1 Tbsp. vinegar
2 Tbsp. Worcestershire sauce

2 Tbsp. Tabasco
1 Tbsp. creole seasoning

SHRIMP STUFFING

2 large shrimp
1 cup fancy lump crabmeat
½ cup red bell pepper, chopped finely
½ cup celery, diced

¼ cup purple onion, chopped
¼ cup Italian bread crumbs
1 lemon, sliced
2 Tbsp. Tabasco sauce
1 tsp. mayonnaise

Boil and peel shrimp, then marinate shrimp in mix above. Slice back of shrimp and stuff with all ingredients. Bake at 350 degrees for 15 minutes.

Kristin Duke

SEARED SALMON with TOMATO, LEEKS and ARTICHOKE

5 - 6 oz. salmon fillets, skin off
2 Tbsp. olive oil
2 tsp. garlic, minced
1 cup of ⅛ wedge artichoke hearts
½ cup leeks, fine julienne

¾ cup diced tomatoes, ¼ inch
4 oz. white wine
4 oz. fish stock or clam juice
3 Tbsp. butter
2 Tbsp. basil, fine julienne
1 tsp. salt and pepper mixture

Sear salmon fillets until golden brown and finish in the oven. When done cooking place salmon on a platter and keep warm. In a pan heat olive oil. Add garlic, artichokes, leeks and tomatoes and sauté for 2 minutes. Add white wine and reduce by half. Add fish stock and again reduce by half. Whip in soft butter to thicken. Season with salt and pepper and garnish with fresh julienne basil. When serving, ladle sauce over salmon.

Boxwood Bistro

Breakfast Casseroles

Here are three delicious variations on the same theme.

ROSIE'S HAM and EGG BAKE

I am submitting a recipe that my mother has passed down to my sisters and me, and that we love to make when we are all able to get together for breakfast or brunch, which is not very often any more since I am here and they are all in Northern Michigan. It's a pretty basic breakfast casserole, but it is still one of the best I've ever tasted. It makes a wonderful holiday breakfast, or a delicious addition to a midday brunch before a Titans football game. The best thing is that it is assembled the evening before and refrigerated overnight. Just pop in the oven the next morning.

PS: When my mother visited from Michigan last year I took her to Carnton for the tour. She had just finished reading The Widow of the South, *so she became my own personal tour guide as we roamed the grounds. Since then (at the age of 79) she has become a master gardener, so I need to get her back down here for another tour in the spring so she can view the vintage gardens!*

French bread baguette
1 lb. cooked ham
½ lb. sharp cheddar cheese, cubed
3 eggs
2 cups milk
½ tsp. dry mustard
½ tsp. salt
1 stick butter, melted

Cube enough bread to cover the bottom of a 13 x 9 inch oven proof baking dish. Top with the cubed ham and cheese. Beat eggs, mustard and salt into the milk, then pour over the layers in the dish.

Pour the melted butter over all. Cover and refrigerate overnight. Preheat oven to 325 degrees. Uncover casserole and bake for one hour.

Diane Payne

BREAKFAST CASSEROLE

2 cups grated sharp cheddar
4 eggs lightly beaten
1 lb. Rudy's Farm hot sausage
¼ cup butter

4 cups water
½ tsp. salt
1 cup Jim Dandy Quick Grits

Preheat oven to 350 degrees. Grease 2 qt. glass baking dish. Brown sausage and drain. Bring water and salt to boil. Stir in grits. Cover and reduce heat to low, stirring occasionally. Cool 5 minutes.

Remove from heat. Stir in butter and only 1 cup of cheddar cheese, until melted. Stir in eggs and sausage. Pour into glass baking dish, Sprinkle top with remaining cheese. May need a little extra. Bake 40 - 45 minutes till set.

Cool 10 minutes before serving.

Carole Guthrie

FAVORITE SAUSAGE BREAKFAST CASSEROLE

1 lb. sausage
6 slices white bread, crust removed
Softened butter
1 ½ cups shredded cheese, longhorn or cheddar
5 eggs
2 cups half and half
1 tsp. salt
1 tsp. dry mustard

Cook and crumble sausage. Drain on paper towel. Spread butter on bread and place in 13 x 9 casserole dish, sprayed with Pam. Sprinkle with sausage, top with cheese. Combine remaining ingredients and beat well. Pour over mixture in dish and chill 8 hours or overnight. Bake at 350 degrees for 40 - 50 minutes.

Joan Young

Carrie and John McGavock's children Winder and Hattie are pictured here about ages 5 and 8.

Vegetables and Side Dishes

Nineteenth century innovations such as canning, processing, chemical preserving and shipping brought convenience into the kitchen. While one can appreciate the time saving such advances meant to the average exhausted "a man may work from dawn to dusk but a woman's work is never done" housewife, the unintended consequence was that fresh foods became less common in many kitchens. Additionally, farmers stopped producing produce varieties that although tasty, bruised easily in transport. Nowadays, some gardeners and farmers search out seeds from old cultivars and grow again the luscious old varieties.

CHOWCHOW

Carrie McGavock's recipe for this vegetable relish appeared in the Tennessee Model Household Guide. *She noted, "Will keep for years."*

2 peck green cucumbers
½ peck green tomatoes
1 pint of green peppers
½ peck of onions
1 ounce of celery seed
1 ounce of white mustard seed
1 ounce of turmeric

1 ounce of whole cloves
3 tablespoonfuls of ground mustard
Grated horse radish and black pepper to taste
2 pounds of brown sugar

Slice or chop fine, *salt well*, and hang in thin cloth to drip *in eve*; next morning *scald* in weak vinegar, then squeeze, dry, and add strong vinegar.

Carrie McGavock

EDISTO TOMATO PIE

1 - 9 in. deep dish pie shell, pre-baked at 375 degrees for 10 minutes
5 large tomatoes, peeled and thickly sliced
½ tsp. salt
½ tsp. black pepper
3 tsp. dried basil
Garlic pepper to taste
¾ cup mayonnaise
1 ¼ cup grated cheddar cheese

Combine salt, pepper, basil and garlic powder. Layer tomatoes in pie shell sprinkling each layer with spices above. Combine mayonnaise and cheese then spread over the tomatoes. Bake at 350 degrees for 35 minutes, or until golden brown and bubbly. Let stand for 5 minutes before serving.

Variations: add 1 chopped onion to mayonnaise and cheese mix. Top with herb dressing rather than mayonnaise and cheese mixture or mix bacon chips with the topping mixture.

Nancy Hippensteel

GRITS CASSEROLE

4 ½ cups boiling water
1 tsp. salt
1 cup grits
1 stick of butter
1 cup cheese
⅔ cup milk
1 roll garlic cheese
2 eggs

Boil water, salt and grits for 15 - 20 minutes. Add butter and 1 cup of cheese to mixture. Beat eggs and add milk to make 1 cup of liquid. Stir into grits mixture and place in greased 2 quart casserole dish. Bake at 350 degrees for 1 ½ hours.

Carole Guthrie

AUNT VICKY'S GREEN BEANS

Sister-in-law Vicky Gould served these years ago and they've been known forever to my kids as Aunt Vicky's Green Beans.

1 lb. green snap beans
3 fresh garlic cloves, minced
2 tsp. kosher salt
2 Tbsp. olive oil

Steam beans in one inch water just until the color changes. Drain water, drizzle with olive oil, salt and garlic. Mix thoroughly.

Serve hot, or delicious the next day chilled.

Margie Thessin

SWEET POTATO PUDDING

My mother Jane Lehew Peay has served this at family meals for as long as I can remember. She was given the recipe by her mother, Leola Lehew. We have always had it with the meal but it is great with whipped cream or vanilla ice cream later that evening after recovering from a holiday feast.

4 cups sweet potatoes, grated
1 ⅓ cups milk
⅓ cup butter, melted
1 ½ cups sugar
4 eggs, beaten
½ tsp. allspice
½ tsp. cinnamon

Peel and grate the sweet potatoes. Stir in milk so the potatoes will not darken. Add melted butter and stir in other ingredients. Stir well and pour into a greased 9 x 13 glass baking dish. Bake for 1 hour or until firm in a 350 degree oven.

Rod Pewitt

MISS GENEVA'S BEST CORN CASSEROLE YOU EVER HAD

1 can whole corn
1 can cream-style corn
3 eggs
½ cup of whole milk
2 Tbsp. of sugar
1 stick of butter
2 Tbsp. flour

Mix the sugar, flour, milk & eggs together and then beat it. Melt butter in casserole dish in the oven. Do NOT brown it. Pour butter back into the mix and add the corn and pour the mix back in the casserole dish. Cook at 400 degrees for 30 minutes or until brown on top. Cook a little longer if it's too soupy. This recipe can be doubled.

Robert Hicks

OLIVE-RICE CASSEROLE

This is my favorite recipe of all time. So quick. So delicious. So nutritious.

1 cup brown rice, uncooked
1 cup tomatoes, canned, diced
1 cup New York state cheese
½ cup onion, chopped
⅓ cup light salad oil
2 oz. of stuffed olives, sliced
1 cup water
Salt and pepper to taste

Combine all ingredients and bake in covered casserole for 1 hour at 350 degrees. Ingredients will be soupy at first, but the rice will absorb the moisture. This is a delicious buffet side dish, or add solid, cubed tofu (about 1 cup or more) for a delightful all-veggie main dish.

Hope V. Hallum

ASPARAGUS SOUFFLE

1 medium bunch asparagus, about 8 oz.
⅓ cup cheddar cheese, finely shredded
⅓ cup mayonnaise
¼ cup onion, chopped
1 egg white

Preheat oven to 350 degrees. Lightly steam asparagus until it is just tender, approximately 5 minutes. Cut spears into bite-sized pieces. In a bowl, combine the asparagus, cheese, mayonnaise and onion. In a small mixing bowl, beat egg white on medium speed until soft peaks form. Fold into asparagus mixture. Transfer to greased 2 ½ quart baking dish. Bake, uncovered, at 350 degrees for 20 - 25 minutes or until lightly browned.

Ginny Holley

VEGETABLE MARINADE

1 can tiny peas
1 can French green beans
1 can shoepeg corn (white)
1 small jar pimento
1 can mushrooms, sliced
1 cup onion, chopped
1 cup green pepper, chopped
1 cup sugar
¾ cup vinegar
½ cup oil
1 tsp. water

Drain all vegetables. Bring sugar, vinegar, oil, water, salt and pepper to boil. Cool and pour over vegetables. Refrigerate. Keeps up to 2 weeks.

Ellen DiLorenzo

AUTUMN PUMPKIN TUREEN

1 pie pumpkin (4 lb.) washed and dried
2 Tbsp. vegetable oil
2 cloves garlic, minced
6 oz. shredded Swiss cheese
4 slices white bread, toasted and crumbled
2 oz. shredded mozzarella
1 pt. half and half
1 tsp. salt
½ tsp. pepper
½ tsp. fresh ground nutmeg

Preheat oven to 350 degrees. Cut 2 inch slice from top of pumpkin and reserve. Remove seeds and fibers. Blend oil and garlic and rub inside of pumpkin, place in a large roasting pan. Alternate layers of toast crumbs and cheeses inside pumpkin. Combine half and half, salt, pepper and nutmeg and pour over layers. Replace top and bake pumpkin for two hours, gently stirring contents after 1 ½ hours. Serve with French bread fingers or Fritos scoops.

Ginny Holley

BROCCOLI and RICE CASSEROLE

1 ½ sticks butter
1 cup finely chopped onion
2 bunches fresh broccoli
1 cup rice (not instant)
2 cans cream of chicken soup
¾ large jar Cheez-Whiz

Cook broccoli florets until tender. Sauté onion in butter. Cook rice as directed on package. Combine all ingredients well and place in 9 x 13 baking dish that has been sprayed with Pam. Bake at 350 degrees for 30 minutes.

Jo Ann Yancy

ZUCCHINI and YELLOW SQUASH CASSEROLE

2 lb. squash (yellow and zucchini combined), sliced
¼ cup onion, minced
2 cups cheddar and Monterey Jack cheese, grated
1 - 10 oz. can Rotel tomatoes and chilies, diced and drained
2 Tbsp. sugar
¾ cup butter
1 tsp. salt
¼ tsp. black pepper
1½ cups cracker crumbs

Boil squash and onion until tender. Drain. Add cheese, tomatoes and chilies, sugar, ½ cup butter, salt and pepper. Pour into 2 quart casserole; drizzle with remaining ¼ cup butter.

Top with cracker crumbs. Bake at 350 degrees for 30 minutes.

Marilyn Lehew

SQUASH CASSEROLE

10 lbs. yellow squash, chopped
1 large onion, diced
2 Tbsp. margarine
1 Tbsp. sugar
Salt and pepper

Boil for 45 minutes.

Sauté the onion with margarine for 5 minutes. Mash the squash. Add remaining ingredients. Place in a baking dish.

Bake at 375 degrees for 40 minutes. Cover with bread crumbs and toast for 5 minutes.

Puckett's Grocery

Three generations of Winder women: Martha Grundy Winder, Hattie McGavock Cowan and Carrie Winder McGavock.

VEGETABLE, FETA and SWISS CHEESE PIE

1 - 15 in. square unbaked lavosh (cracker bread); if not available you may use 2 - 9 in. unbaked pie shells. If using lavosh line it into a greased 12 in. tart pan, cut and trim sides.
5 eggs, separated
1 cup heavy cream
1 Tbsp. onion, minced
½ tsp. basil
¼ tsp. marjoram
¼ tsp. black pepper
1 ½ cup frozen chopped spinach, well drained
2 cups coarsely grated carrots, yellow squash and zucchini
1 ½ cup Swiss cheese, shredded
½ cup feta cheese

Beat egg yolks with cream, onion and herbs. Beat egg whites in separate bowl until stiff. Fold egg yolk mixture into beaten egg whites. Place grated vegetables in bottom of crust. Top with spinach and cheeses. Gently pour egg mixture into shell. Bake in pre-heated 375 degree oven 40 - 50 minutes, or until set.

Marilyn Lehew

TOMATO-OKRA CASSEROLE

1 egg
½ cup fresh broken bread, packed
¼ cup butter, melted
¼ tsp. garlic, chopped

¼ cup onion, chopped
1 Tbsp. sugar
¼ tsp. pepper
1 can diced tomatoes in juice
¼ lb. fresh okra, thinly sliced

Beat egg in mixing bowl. Add bread crumbs, butter, garlic, onion, sugar, pepper. Let sit 2 to 3 minutes. Add tomatoes and okra. Pour into greased shallow baking dish. Bake at 350 degrees for 20 minutes. Top with parmesan cheese. Return to oven for an additional 5 minutes.

Marilyn Lehew

AUNT FANNY'S BAKED SQUASH

3 lbs. yellow summer squash, cut up
½ cup onion, chopped
½ cup bread crumbs
2 eggs
1 stick butter
1 Tbsp. sugar
1 tsp. salt
½ tsp. black pepper

Boil squash in small amount of salted water until tender, about 15 - 20 minutes. Drain and mash. Add all ingredients except half the butter and bread crumbs to squash.

Pour mixture in deep baking dish. Spread remaining melted butter over top. Add crumbs. Bake at 375 degrees for 1 hour.

Ellen DiLorenzo

FRIED GREEN TOMATOES

I wasn't a fan of fried green tomatoes until I tried them at the Blue Willow Inn in Social Circle, Georgia. Now I have them wherever they're served.

¾ cup flour
¼ cup cornmeal
¼ tsp. salt
¼ tsp. pepper
¾ cup milk
3 - 4 green tomatoes, sliced
Vegetable oil

Combine flour, cornmeal, salt, pepper and mix thoroughly. Dip tomato slices into batter and fry in 2 inches hot oil. A heavy cast iron skillet is best. Brown on one side, then turn and brown on the other.

Margie Thessin

TOMATO TART

One of the pleasures of living on Carnton Lane for many years was the accessibility of Carnton Plantation and the Confederate Cemetery. We always entertained guests with a walk that ended on the grounds. Later when the gardens were first planted and it was permissible, my husband and I would include a stroll through the vegetable gardens admiring the design, the beautiful vegetables and especially the tomatoes. My dad, in Alabama, was supplying us with his own crop of prize-winning Big Boys, so I was often motivated to come home and bake something like this tomato tart.

CRUST

1 ½ cups all-purpose flour
½ tsp. fine sea salt
10 Tbsp. butter

¼ tsp. fresh lemon juice
6 - 8 Tbsp. ice cold water

Sift together flour and salt. Cut in butter, add lemon juice and water gradually until the dough just comes together. (Try 6 tablespoons water first; only add the other 2 if you need them!) Be careful not to over mix. Turn out onto a floured surface. Shape dough into a disk and wrap in plastic wrap. Refrigerate till dough is firm, about 1 hour. Then roll on a lightly floured surface to ¼ inch thickness and line a removable bottom tart pan. Chill again for 15 minutes. Partially bake the tart shell. Line the pan with parchment paper and fill with pie weights or beans. Bake until the dough is set and dried but not brown, about 10-15 minutes. Remove pie weights and bake for 5 more minutes. Remove from oven and cool 10 minutes.

TART

2 Tbsp. Dijon mustard
8 oz. (2 cups) grated gruyere cheese
3 large red ripe tomatoes

3 Tbsp. extra virgin olive oil
1 tsp. fine sea salt
½ tsp ground black pepper
1 Tbsp. fresh basil chopped

Spread the tart with mustard and then the grated cheese. Arrange tomatoes in an overlapping pattern and drizzle with olive oil. Season with salt and pepper. Bake until pie crust is browned, about 30 minutes. Top with chopped basil. Serve warm or at room temperature.

Gwen King

CARROT SOUFFLE

This recipe was a favorite of my Great-Grandmother. She called it "Mystery Pie" so she could get my Grandfather to eat more vegetables!

1 lb. carrots, peeled and sliced
½ cup melted butter
3 eggs
1 cup sugar
3 Tbsp. flour
1 tsp. flour
1 tsp. vanilla extract

Boil carrots until tender, drain. Add butter and blend (in a blender) until smooth. Add remaining ingredients. Blend. Pour mixture into a 1 quart casserole or soufflé dish. Bake at 350 degrees for 45 minutes or until firm.

Joanna Stephens

MONELL'S CORN CASSEROLE

½ stick margarine or butter
6 eggs, lightly beaten
1 cup sugar
3 Tbsp. self-rising flour
1 cup milk
3 cans creamed corn

Preheat oven to 350 degrees. Place ½ stick butter in a 2 qt. casserole dish and place in preheated oven. Heat dish until butter melts and starts to bubble. In mixing bowl, combine eggs and sugar and mix lightly. Add flour and milk to egg mixture and mix lightly. Combine corn with the egg mixture and mix lightly. The secret to this recipe is not to over-mix the mixture. Mix lightly, just enough to combine ingredients.

Place corn pudding in hot buttered casserole dish. Leave uncovered and cook for 25 to 30 minutes or until pudding "crowns" and is lightly brown. (Don't make this ahead of time.)

Monell's Restaurant, Bridge Street, Downtown Franklin

BROILED ASPARAGUS

This is so easy to make from ingredients you can keep on hand.

2 cans asparagus
2 Tbsp. butter, melted
Fresh parmesan cheese, grated

Spread asparagus on a broiler-safe pan, pour butter over asparagus, then sprinkle cheese. Broil just until cheese begins to melt. Also a delicious way to enjoy tomatoes.

Margie Thessin

Coconut cake looks delectable on Carrie McGavock's cake stand. The dining table is also original to the house.

The old Paris porcelain china is from descendants of the Lysander McGavocks, who built Midway Plantation in Brentwood.

Desserts

Prior to the rise of the middle class in the mid-19ᵗʰ century, desserts and sweets made with sugar were enjoyed only by the very wealthy. In Kentucky and Tennessee, the landed gentry protected their precious sugar under lock and key in a regionally unique piece of furniture called the sugar chest. For others, dessert could be something as simple as dried apples or molasses on rice. Sweetened biscuits, which became known as cookies, also became popular during this time. Although often reserved for special meals or events, cakes and pies and any kinds of desserts were treasured parts of the 19ᵗʰ century meal.

TRANSPARENT PUDDING

From the Tennessee Model Household Guide, *another recipe from Mrs. C.W. McG, Franklin, Tenn.*

Yolks of 10 eggs, white of 2 eggs, 1 pound of sugar, ½ pound of fresh butter, season with nutmeg or lemon.

Make your pastry (you may put a layer of citron, pineapple, or any kind of fruit on it), and pour mixture over it. Bake, and then beat whites of eggs, adding white sugar to stiffen, and pour over, and bake for a few minutes.

Carrie McGavock

CHOCOLATE CUP CAKES

1 ½ cups flour, sifted
1 ½ tsp. baking powder
½ tsp. salt
⅓ cup butter
1 cup sugar
2 eggs, well beaten
1 tsp. vanilla
½ cup milk
2 sq. Baker's chocolate (unsweetened), melted and cooled

Sift flour once, measure, add baking powder and salt, and sift together three times. Cream butter thoroughly, then add sugar, gradually, and cream together until light and fluffy. Add eggs and vanilla and beat well. Add flour, alternately with milk, a small amount at a time. Beat after each addition until smooth. Fold in chocolate. Pour into greased muffin pans. Bake in moderate oven 15 minutes. These can be iced if desired.

Harriet Ayres Smith, daughter of Hattie McGavock Ayres and sister of Susie Mai Ayres Heller.

BOILED MOLASSES PUDDING

James McGavock left County Antrim, Northern Ireland in the mid-1700s and settled at Fort Chiswell, in Wythe County, Virginia. Randal, one of James's 11 children, headed over the mountains to Tennessee in 1796. The McGavock name is still prominent in parts of Virginia.

1 cupful of molasses
1 cupful of sweet milk
4 cupfuls of sifted flour
1 cupful of stoned raisins

½ cupful of butter
1 teaspoonful of soda
1 teaspoonful of salt

Boil or steam in a pudding mould. Eat with wine sauce.

Mrs. McGavock of Pulaski County, Virginia

MATTIE JACKSON HICKS'S BEST LEMON ICE CREAM

1 cup sugar
Rind of 2 lemons, finely grated
⅛ tsp. salt
3 Tbsp. lemon juice
1 cup heavy whipping cream
1 cup half and half

Combine rind, juice and sugar and mix evenly. Gradually stir in cream, half and half and salt. Mix well. Put into tray and freeze for 1 - 2 hours Stir well with wooden spoon and refreeze.

Robert Hicks

PECAN BALLS

This simple recipe reaches back to the 1870s.

1 cup butter
½ cup sifted powdered sugar
1½ tsp. vanilla
2 ½ cups all-purpose flour
1 cup pecans, finely chopped
Powdered sugar

Beat butter for 30 seconds. Add ½ cup of powdered sugar and the vanilla; beat till fluffy. Beat in flour; stir in pecans.

Roll into 1-inch balls and bake on ungreased baking sheets at 300 degrees for 18 - 20 minutes. Cool on wire racks. Shake in powdered sugar in brown bag. Makes 60.

Robert Hicks

STRAWBERRY PIE

1 cup sugar
3 Tbsp. cornstarch
¼ tsp. salt
1 Tbsp. lemon juice
½ cup water
2 cups strawberries, halved

Mash above ingredients (except the strawberries) together in bowl and cook on high in microwave for seven minutes stirring every two minutes.

Pour over 2 cups halved strawberries in baked pie shell. Chill before serving.

This is best when eaten the same day it is made.

Lucy Battle

NANY'S BUTTERMILK POUND CAKE

3 cups sugar
½ cup vegetable shortening (Crisco)
1 stick margarine, softened
5 eggs
½ tsp. soda dissolved in 1 Tbsp. boiling water
1 cup buttermilk
3 cups sifted plain flour
½ tsp. salt
2 tsp. vanilla

Cream sugar, vegetable shortening and margarine together. Add eggs and mix well. Next add soda dissolved in water, then add buttermilk. Add flour alternately with milk and mix well with a mixer. Pour mixture into a tall stem cake pan that has been greased with Crisco. Bake at 300 degrees for about 1 hour or until done. Check with toothpick.

Joan Young

ITALIAN CREAM CAKE

This Italian Cream Cake is delightful for the holidays. It can be refrigerated for a month or frozen until ready to use. The recipe is in Recipes from Miss Daisy's.

CAKE

¼ cup butter, softened
½ cup shortening (Crisco)
2 cups granulated sugar
5 eggs, separated
2 cups all-purpose flour
1 tsp. baking soda
1 cup buttermilk
1 tsp. vanilla extract
1 - 4 oz. can coconut
1 cup pecans, chopped

In large bowl or mixer, mix butter and shortening. Add sugar, beat until smooth. Add egg yolks one at a time, beating well after each. Combine flour and soda, add to creamed mixture, alternately with buttermilk. Stir in vanilla, coconut and pecans. Beat egg whites until still and gently fold into batter. Pour into 3 greased 8 inch cake pans. Bake in a 350 degree oven for 20-25 minutes. Cool.

FROSTING

1 - 8 oz. pkg. cream cheese, softened
4 Tbsp. butter, softened
1 - 1 lb. confectioner's sugar
1 tsp. vanilla extract
2 Tbsp. evaporated milk
 Pecans, chopped

In large bowl or mixer, combine all frosting ingredients except pecans. Beat to a spreading consistency. Spread between layers and on top of cake. Sprinkle pecans on top.

Miss Daisy King

LILLIAN JACKSON JONES' POUND CAKE

This is adapted from her mother's 19th century recipe.

½ pound of softened butter
1 ⅔ cups of sugar
5 eggs
2 cups flour
1 teaspoon pure vanilla extract
1 teaspoon almond extract

Bake at 275 degrees in cake pan for 60 - 75 minutes.

Robert Hicks

MATTIE JACKSON HICKS'
MOTHER OF ALL CHESS PIES

This recipe is adapted from her grandmother's recipe (then called custard pie) brought to Middle Tennessee from Philadelphia when she married in the 1830s. By all accounts, this custard pie was the first to be called "chess pie."

FILLING (for a 9-inch single crust pie)

1 cup sugar
¼ cup butter
½ cup heavy whipping cream
1 Tbsp. corn meal
2 whole eggs
1 tsp. lemon flavoring
1 tsp. pure vanilla extract

Mix all the above in a mixer and pour into uncooked pie crust.

Cook about 20 minutes at 400 - 425 degrees then reduce the temperature to about 300 - 325 degrees. Cook about 30 - 35 minutes more until the crust and the top of the filling are brown.

Robert Hicks

LINDA'S COCONUT CAKE

1 box butter flavored cake mix
2 cups sugar
1 - 16 oz. carton sour cream
1 - 12 oz. pkg. coconut
1 - 8 oz. carton whipped topping

Prepare cake mix according to directions on package. Bake in 2 round cake pans. Cool. Slice each layer in half (use wire cake cutter or thread). Combine sugar, sour cream and coconut. Mix well and chill. Spread coconut mixture on layers, reserving 1 cup. Mix whipped topping with remaining coconut mixture and frost sides and top. Keep refrigerated. Better if made 2 or 3 days in advance. Freezes well.

Joan Young

GINGER COOKIES

2 cups flour, plain
1 cup sugar
1 tsp. cinnamon
½ tsp. ground cloves
½ tsp. ginger
½ tsp. salt
2 tsp. baking soda

Mix well. Then add:

¾ cups oil
¼ cup molasses
1 egg

Pour into dry ingredients. Mix and form into balls. Roll in sugar and place on cookie sheet and bake for 10 minutes at 350 degrees.

Candie Westbrook

GOLDEN LEMON BUTTER

This keeeps for weeks in refrigerator. And is so easy and good. Fill baked tart shells and top with whipped cream (not Cool Whip - they are nothing but sugar & butter so go the whole way to make them delicious.)

6 eggs plus 2 yolks
2 cups sugar
Rind and juice of 4 lemons
1 cup butter

Stir beaten eggs and sugar together in top of double boiler. Add lemon rind, juice and butter. Cook over gently boiling water, stirring frequently until mixture is as smooth and thick as mayonnaise. Remove from heat and cool. Makes 2 pints (12 - 14 tarts).

Anne Rutherford

TUTTI-FRUITY HOMEMADE ICE CREAM

3 cups milk
3 cups cream
3 cups sugar
Juice of 3 lemons
Juice of 3 oranges
3 bananas, mashed

Combine only milk, cream and sugar. Stir until dissolved. Place in an ice cream freezer and freeze until thoroughly chilled with a mushy consistency.

Add the combined fruit juices and bananas.

Continue freezing until firm. Remove the dasher, serve immediately or freeze in airtight container. Makes 1 gallon.

Nena Manci

PEACH AND BLUEBERRY CRISP

This crisp is a recipe I found in a magazine years ago and tried it for my family. It was an immediate hit and is often requested for back porch family dinners in the summer time. With a scoop of home-made vanilla ice cream what could be better on a hot summer day!

TOPPING

¾ cup firmly packed brown sugar
¾ cup all-purpose flour
½ cup unsalted butter, cut into pieces
1 cup old-fashioned oats
¾ cup pecans, chopped

Preheat oven to 350 degrees. Butter a 9 x 13 x 2 glass baking dish. Mix sugar and flour in medium bowl. Add butter and rub with fingers until mixture resembles coarse crumbs. Mix in oats and pecans.

FRUIT

6 Tbsp. sugar
3 Tbsp. all purpose flour
½ tsp. ground cinnamon
⅛ tsp. ground nutmeg
3 ½ lbs. peaches, peeled and each cut into 6 wedges
1 pt. blueberries

Mix sugar, flour, cinnamon and nutmeg in large bowl. Add peaches and blueberries and toss to coat.

Transfer fruit to prepared dish. Sprinkle topping over fruit. Bake until topping browns and filling bubbles, about 45 minutes.

Serve warm with vanilla ice cream or yogurt.

Margaret Roberts

CHARLOTTE RUSSE

This is an old McGavock Receipe. We always use our McGavock family clear-cut crystal bowl to serve. This recipe takes time, but we dare not have Thanksgiving or Christmas without it!

3 eggs, separated
½ cup sugar
2 cups milk
Pinch of salt
1 envelope Knox gelatin
¼ cup cold water
1 ½ Tbsp. vanilla
6 Tbsp. sugar (for egg whites)
½ pt. whipping cream
2 Tbsp. sugar

Use top of double boiler. Beat yolks slightly, beat in sugar (do not beat much). Stir in milk. Mix well. Cook over hot water, until custard coats spoon, stirring frequently for about 15 minutes.

Meanwhile, stir gelatin in cold water, then dissolve well over hot water. When custard is done, add gelatin; mix well. Add vanilla and mix again. Set in refrigerator to cool. Stir frequently.

When custard has cooled, beat egg whites in crock with rotary beater. Gradually put in 6 tablespoons of sugar. Whip until it "piles" not stiff.

Transfer egg whites to large bowl. Slowly fold in thickened, cooled custard until well mixed. Again in crock with rotary beater, whip cream (add 2 tablespoons sugar until it "piles"). Gently fold into custard mixture.

Set in refrigerator; continue to fold occasionally (to prevent separation) until it piles softly. If desired, transfer to a serving dish. Just in case it curdles, beat with rotary beater.

Elizabeth McGavock Darby and Mary Margaret Whittle McGavock Cain

CAROLINA TRIFFLE

Triffle *is a regional spelling for the more-commonly known* trifle, *although either way the pronunciation is the same.*

½ lb. pound cake, cut into bit size pieces
1 small box vanilla pudding
½ cup milk
⅓ cup sherry
Whipped cream, sweetened to taste

Let pound cake pieces dry out. Prepare pudding as directed plus add ½ cup extra milk. Add sherry to mixed pudding. Repeat until all is used and chill. Top with a cherry.

May be layered in individual dishes or parfaits for serving.

Becky Darby

MATTIE JACKSON HICKS' MOTHER'S BOILED CUSTARD C.1880

Mattie Jackson Hicks was a Methodist so there was no acknowledged alcohol added. You know what's right, so do it.

3 qts. whole milk
2 ½ cups sugar
Pinch of salt
6 Tbsp. cornstarch
10 egg yolks plus 10 whole eggs, beaten

Warm the milk in a double boiler. Combine sugar, salt and cornstarch with beaten yolks and then the beaten whole eggs. Slowly add the warm milk so as not to cook the eggs. Continually stir, stir, stir about 15 minutes until it thickens and "coats the spoon."

Robert Hicks

VERNA'S CHEESECAKE

CRUST

1½ sticks butter, melted
6 heaping Tbsp. sugar
1½ cups flour

Mix thoroughly into piecrust consistency. Line cheesecake pan with aluminum foil, make sure the sides are even. Press piecrust in bottom of pan and around the sides. Preheat oven to 350 degrees.

For Chocolate Crust: add 4 tablespoons of cocoa with the butter and sugar, and use 4 tablespoons less flour.

FILLING

3 - 8 oz. pkgs. Philadelphia
Brand cream cheese, softened
1 cup sugar

4 large eggs
¼ cup whipping cream

Mix cream cheese and sugar until creamy. Add eggs, one at a time, beating between each egg. Be sure to scrape the sides and bottom of the bowl so it will be thoroughly mixed. Add whipping cream.

For Almond Flavored Cheesecake: Add 1 teaspoon of almond flavoring.

For Peanut Butter Cup Cheesecake: After you bake, immediately add 10 Reese's cups cut up in small pieces to top. It will melt slightly allowing it to stick to the top when cold.

For Coconut Cheesecake: ½ teaspoon of coconut flavoring. Pour the filling into the crust, top cake with sweetened coconut as desired and top with chopped pecans. I usually press this down somewhat into the batter with my fingers.

For Oreo Cheesecake: Original batter recipe, pour half into crust, pulverize ¾ - 1 cup of Oreo cookies and sprinkle over batter, top with remaining batter. When cheesecake is finished, and cold, ice entire cheesecake with semi-sweet icing (recipe below- don't add almond flavoring).

For Chocolate Cheesecake: Melt about 1 cup milk chocolate chips and add the chocolate mixture to the cheesecake batter.

For Turtle Cheesecake: Add chopped milk chocolate to top, add a good brand of chopped dark chocolate on top of that, or mini semi-sweet chips and top off with chopped pecans and press all down slightly with spoon.

Pour filling into crust and bake. The time is always iffy. I set my timer at 45 minutes, just to check the top of the cake. It shouldn't be very brown. Then I check it every 5 minutes, it may be done at 50 minutes, but it may not be done until 55 minutes or 1 hour. If the top starts getting brown, I put a piece of aluminum foil over the top of the pan, try not to touch the foil to the cake. The cake is done when it jiggles just a bit in the middle. I let my cake cool in the refrigerator overnight. Then I remove the sides, peel off the aluminum foil and slide the cake onto a plate. You can add cherry pie filling, or drizzle icing over it.

ICING

Heat ½ cup whipping cream in microwave about a minute. Add a teensy bit of almond flavoring, maybe ¼ of a capful of the flavoring. You just want a hint of the flavoring. Add 1 ¼ cups of semi-sweet chocolate chips and then let them melt. You want it to harden up when it is refrigerated, but soft enough to drizzle. Add chopped nuts to this mixture, and then drizzle the icing over the top and sides of the cheesecake.

CARAMEL SAUCE

Melt 1 stick of butter with 1 cup of sugar, stirring occasionally to let caramelize. When light brown, remove from heat, add one cup of whipping cream, stirring constantly and quickly (be careful this causes a great amount of steam and you can get burned!).

Deborah Faulkner

POLLY HICKS' GRANDMOTHER'S CUSTARD

1 gallon whole milk

16 eggs

1¾ cups sugar

2 Tbsp. vanilla

1 orange

1 pt. heavy whipping cream

½ tsp. nutmeg

Scald milk in large double boiler or a large pan set in a larger pan filled with boiling water.

Beat eggs until 'lemony' and add sugar as you beat them. Add egg/sugar mix to the scalding milk and cook over medium heat. Stir with a wooden spoon until mixture coats the spoon (approximately 20 minutes) Add vanilla and nutmeg. Add the juice of a whole orange and stir. Strain into a jug or pitcher, cover & refrigerate for at least 4 hours. The custard may be frozen and eaten as frozen custard or simply cooled and served as boiled custard. Add alcohol at will. Without alcohol this makes 35 to 40 servings.

Robert Hicks

BLUE RIBBON BLUEBERRY PIE

1 - 8 oz. pkg. cream cheese, room temperature

2 cups powdered sugar

1 can blueberry pie filling

12 oz. Cool Whip

2 pie shells

½ cup crushed pecans

Cover bottom of pie shells with crushed pecans before baking, then bake and cool shells as directed.

Mix cream cheese and powdered sugar. Layer onto the pie shell, beginning with the pie filling, then add the cream cheese and sugar mix, then the Cool Whip. Repeat for the next layer, making sure Cool Whip is on the very top.

Ona B. Faulkner

MOLASSES COOKIES

Ruth Akin Hackman was a native of Burwood, in western Williamson County. Her father in 1911 built the store known as Huff's Grocery that still operates today.

1 cup sugar	2 tsp. baking soda
1 egg	1 tsp. salt
¼ cup molasses	1 tsp. allspice
¾ cup peanut or Wesson oil	2 tsp. cinnamon
2 cups flour	

Mix sugar, egg, molasses and oil. Sift together flour, baking soda, salt, allspice and cinnamon, and add to the other ingredients.

If too soft, put in refrigerator for 20 minutes. Roll into balls the size of walnuts. Roll in sugar and place on ungreased cookie sheet. Leave plenty of room to spread.

Bake at 350 degrees for 10 minutes.

Ruth Akin Hackman, submitted by her daughter, Joanna Harris of Amherst, Virginia.

This is just one of almost 200 pieces of Old Paris porcelain in the collection at Carnton.

PUMPKIN PIE BARS

1 ¼ cups flour
¾ cups oats
½ cup packed brown sugar
½ cup chopped pecans
⅔ cup butter, melted
4 eggs

2 - 15 oz. cans solid packed pumpkin
2 - 14 oz. cans sweetened condensed milk
2 tsp. cinnamon
1 tsp. pumpkin pie spice

Heat oven to 350 degrees. Combine flour, oats and brown sugar. Add chopped pecans. Melt butter and add to dry ingredients. Mix well and press mixture into two 11 x 17 inch glass dishes. Bake 15 minutes.

Meanwhile, lightly beat eggs. Add pumpkin, condensed milk and spices. Whisk until smooth and pour over crust. Bake 30 - 35 minutes or until filling is set and knife comes out clean. Let cool and serve with whipping cream. The recipe can be cut in half.

Patti Caprara

SHAKERTOWN CORN PUDDING

From Shakertown, Kentucky

2 cups of corn
2 Tbsp. flour
2 Tbsp. sugar
1 tsp. salt
3 Tbsp. butter
3 whole eggs
1¾ cups of milk

Blend butter, sugar, flour and salt. Add eggs, beating well. Stir in corn and milk. Bake at 350 degrees for 45 minutes to one hour.

Marianne Schroer

APPLE-CRANBERRY CRUMBLE PIE

TOPPING

¾ cup oats
½ cup packed brown sugar
¼ tsp. nutmeg

Dash salt
2 Tbsp. butter, chilled

Cut butter into first 5 ingredients until it resembles a crumble.

FILLING

3 cups apples, sliced
2 cups fresh cranberries

⅔ cup packed brown sugar
2 ½ tsp. cornstarch

Fill pie crust with above mixed filling and top with the crumble mixture. Bake at 350 degrees approximately 1 hour or until brown and bubbly. Cool at least 1 hour.

Gina Olsen

CHESSCAKE SQUARES

1 box yellow cake mix
2 eggs
½ cup margarine, softened

Mix together and press into a greased 9 x 13 pan.

1 - 16 oz. box confectioner's sugar, sifted
1 - 8 oz. pkg. cream cheese, softened
1 tsp. vanilla

Mix together and spread on top of the cake batter. Bake at 350 degrees for 35 – 40 minutes.

Candie Westbrook

BUTTERSCOTCH BROWNIES

My ancestor, Mr. Will Shelton lived at Carnton in the early part of the 20th century.

2 sticks butter, melted
1 box brown sugar (light or dark)
¼ cup plain sugar
4 eggs, beaten
2 ½ cups self-rising flour
1 tsp. vanilla
1¾ cup pecans, chopped

Mix butter with brown sugar and white sugar, add eggs and stir. Then add flour, vanilla and pecans. Stir well and pour into large greased pan and bake in 350 degree oven for about 20 - 25 minutes. Let cool and sprinkle top with confectioner's sugar. Cut into squares.

Mrs. Ed Collins

WALNUT BALLS

John's grandmother made these for him when he was a child. He now makes them every year for our neighborhood Christmas party.

2 cups vanilla wafer crumbs
½ cup sugar
⅛ tsp. salt
½ tsp. cinnamon
1 tsp. lemon juice
½ cup maraschino cherries, chopped
1 cup walnuts, chopped
⅔ cup sweetened condensed milk
Powdered sugar

Combine and roll into balls. Roll in powdered sugar before serving.

Marianne Schroer

MOM'S SUGAR COOKIES

In the 1980s, Carnton Country Club's golf course on a snowy day became a winter wonderland of fun for our two sons, as our backyard hedge opened into the third fairway. After a day of snow sledding and snowball fighting, many of their friends would often end up in our kitchen (shoes and mittens drying by the fire), having hot cocoa and these sugar cookie cutouts in a snowflake or snowman design. I would hear of many fun adventures, and unfortunately of one daring adventure of our younger son where he intended to aim his sled to cross the bridge on the fourth hole, but instead caused him to come sheepishly home to his Mom in wet clothes! These cookies, in their seasonal shapes, have continued to be a favorite at every holiday gathering. Remember to double the recipe. They freeze beautifully.

⅔ cup margarine, softened
¾ cup sugar
1 tsp. vanilla
1 egg
4 tsp. whole milk
2 cups sifted all-purpose flour
1 ½ tsp. baking powder
¼ tsp. salt

Cream the margarine, sugar and vanilla. Add the egg and milk to the above mixture. Sift the flour with the salt and baking powder and mix together with the creamed margarine and sugar. Chill for at least one hour (can be chilled overnight). Roll out on a board sprinkled lightly with flour. Cut into desired shape. Cook at 375 degrees for 6 - 8 minutes. Do not overcook. Cool and ice.

ICING

1 box powdered sugar
3 - 6 Tbsp. warm water
2 tsp. corn syrup (adds a shiny glaze)
⅛ tsp. vanilla

Mix to proper consistency, adding food color for desired hue.

Gwen King

126

FUDGE PIE

It's delicious served slightly warm with a scoop of peppermint ice cream or vanilla bean ice cream.

1 cup sugar
¼ cup sifted plain flour
¼ cup cocoa

Mix all the above ingredients together.

ADD:

1 stick melted butter
1 tsp. vanilla
2 eggs (slightly beaten)

Mix all ingredients well. Pour into unbaked pie shell. Bake at 325 degrees until filling is firm, about 30 - 35 minutes.

JoAnn Yancy

OREO BALLS

1 pkg. Oreos
1 - 8 oz. pkg. cream cheese
Bark chocolate

Crush the Oreos. Put them in a blender, one half sleeve at a time, and blend until they look like coffee grounds. Mix Oreo crumbs and cream cheese. You'll have to use your hands. Form mixture into balls. Melt bark chocolate. Roll Oreo mixture into balls - about walnut size. Cover in melted chocolate, put on cookie sheet covered in waxed paper. Refrigerate unused portion.

Nancy Hippensteel

SUGAR-FREE TRIFLE

1 pkg. sugar-free vanilla pudding
1 container sugar-free Cool Whip
1 sugar-free angel food cake

⅓ cup orange juice
Any fresh fruit – strawberries, peaches, blueberries, cut up

Mix pudding according to package directions. Mix pudding with Cool Whip. Break up angel food cake. Pour orange juice over the top of the cake. Layer cake, pudding, fruit, cake, pudding fruit in trifle bowl.

Nancy Hippensteel

KIM'S CHOCOLATE PIE

CRUST

3 egg whites
½ tsp. cream of tartar

½ cup sugar
½ cup whole pecans

Beat egg whites until foamy. Add cream of tartar, beat until stiff. Gradually add sugar until smooth and glossy. Use to spread on bottom and sides of well-greased pie plate. Do not spread on rim. Hollow out center a little. Sprinkle pecans on bottom. Bake at 275 degrees for one hour. Cool.

FILLING

1 medium pkg. chocolate chips
3 Tbsp. hot water
1 tsp. vanilla
1 cup heavy cream

Melt chocolate in top of double boiler. Stir in water and simmer until thickened. Cool slightly. Add vanilla, then fold in whipped cream. Turn into shell. Chill.

Eat up! Kim Carnes

POORFARM HOLLOW JAM CAKE
WITH CARAMEL ICING

CAKE

2 cups sugar
1 cups butter, softened
4 eggs
2 ½ cups unbleached flour
1 cup buttermilk
1 pint blackberry jam (we always made our own)
½ pound currants (1 ¼ cups)

2 cups pecans, chopped
1 tsp. nutmeg
½ tsp. fresh ground cloves
2 tsp. allspice
2 scant tsp. soda
½ tsp. ground ginger
½ tsp. salt

Cream butter and sugar until fluffy. Add eggs, one at a time. Add jam and nuts. Sift the dry ingredients except for the soda and then mix the dry ingredients with the currants. Add soda to the buttermilk and stir well and add to the sugar and butter and alternate with your flour mixture. Use greased tube pan and put wax paper in the bottom. Grease the wax paper, too. Bake in moderate oven at 350 degrees. The cake will take almost 45 minutes -- then check it.

ICING

1 cup brown sugar
1 stick butter, softened
4 Tbsp. Pet milk
¼ tsp. salt
2 - 3 Tbsp. white Karo syrup
1 ½ tsp. vanilla
Small box caramel icing mix

Mix and cook 2 - 3 minutes stirring constantly. Remove from the heat add ¾ box of caramel icing mix. Beat with an electric mixer until creamy. Then beat by hand to spread on the top of the cake.

Robert Hicks

POORFARM HOLLOW ICE CREAM

2 ½ quarts heavy whipping cream
3 ½ cups sugar
4 teaspoons vanilla
 3 eggs
5 cups fruit or 25 peaches or strawberries, pulverized

Mix well. Add fruit to the cream mix and blend well. Let it set in refrigerator for 2 hours before freezing it in your ice cream freezer.

Robert Hicks

Carnton is magical after a fresh snowfall.

Special Menus

High Tea at Carnton

The Carnton Association was formed in 1977 to restore the historic house to its former splendor. The house had declined over the years, after it was sold out of the McGavock family in 1911. It had been rented over the years and without much repair work done, it was sadly neglected.

Money was scarce in the early days of the Association. Periodically, fundraising projects were held to supplement the needed income. One of the popular fundraising events was the "Christmas High Tea" held in the historic house over the holiday season.

Here are some of the recipes that were used for the High Teas in the 1980s.

BOURBON FRUIT ROLLS

1 lb. vanilla wafers
1 cup candied cherries
1 cup crystallized pineapple
1 cup whole pecans

1 can sweetened condensed milk
¼ cup bourbon or rum or 1 tsp. almond extract
Powdered sugar

Crumble wafers well. Cut cherries in quarters and cut pineapple small. Mix fruits and nuts with wafers and liquor. Mix in remaining ingredients. Shape into rolls about 2 inches in diameter and roll in powdered sugar. Chill thoroughly. Slice into this round with sharp knife. Do not stack. Place wax paper between slices. Ready to serve.

FUDGE

¾ cup margarine
3 cups sugar
1 - 5 oz. can evaporated milk
12 oz. semi-sweet chocolate
chips

1 - 7 oz. jar marshmallow crème
1 cup nuts, chopped
1 tsp. vanilla

Combine sugar, margarine and milk in heavy 3 qt. saucepan. Bring to a full boil, stirring constantly. Boil for five minutes over medium heat, or until candy thermometer reaches 234 degrees, continuing to stir constantly. Remove from heat. Stir in chocolate chips until melted. Add remaining ingredients. Mix well till blended.

Pour into a greased 9 x 13 pan. Let cool. Cut into one inch squares.

HOT CHICKEN SALAD

2 cups cooked chicken, diced
2 cups celery, chopped
½ cup pecans, finely chopped
1 cup mayonnaise
2 hard-cooked eggs, chopped

½ tsp. salt
2 tsp. onion, finely chopped
2 Tbsp. lemon juice
½ cup Swiss cheese, grated

Chop all ingredients fine and mix well.

CUCUMBER SANDWICHES

White bread
Cucumbers, sliced thin, unpeeled
Radishes, sliced thin, unpeeled
Mayonnaise
Parsley

Cut 2 inch rounds from bread. Slice cucumbers very thin. Place cucumber on a round, with a dab of mayonnaise. Place radish on cucumber, a dab of mayonnaise on top. Crown with a pinch of parsley.

SPRITZ COOKIES

1 cup butter
⅔ cup sugar
3 egg yolks
1 tsp. almond extract
2 ½ cups flour
Food coloring

Heat oven to 400 degrees. Mix butter, sugar, egg yolks, and flavorings thoroughly. Work in flour. Tint the dough either red or green. Using a quarter of the dough at a time, force dough through a cookie press using spiral or poinsettia discs. Bake 7 - 10 minutes or until set but not brown.

THUMBPRINT COOKIES

1 cup shortening
½ cup brown sugar, packed
2 eggs, separated
1 tsp. vanilla

2 cups flour
½ tsp. salt
1½ cups nuts, finely chopped
Jelly, any kind

Heat oven to 350 degrees. Mix shortening, sugar, egg yolks and vanilla thoroughly. Blend flour and salt, stir into shortening mixture. Roll dough into balls (1 teaspoon per ball). Beat egg whites slightly with fork. Dip balls in egg whites. Roll in nuts. Place about one inch apart on ungreased baking sheet; press thumb gently in center of each. Bake 10 - 15 minutes or until set. Fill thumbprints with jelly of your choice.

SPICED TEA

¾ cup instant tea
2 cups sugar
1 lb. 2 oz. size instant orange drink (Tang)

2 tsp. ground cinnamon
1 tsp. ground cloves
1 package unsweetened lemonade mix

Combine all ingredients. Mix well. Store mixture in covered container. To serve, use 2 teaspoons per cup of water (hot or cold). Mix well.

POPPYSEED BREAD

3 cups flour
1 ½ tsp. salt
1 ½ tsp. baking powder
2 ¼ cups sugar
1 ½ tsp. poppy seeds

3 eggs
1 cup oil
1 ½ cups milk
1 ½ tsp. of each: almond,
vanilla, butter flavorings

Combine flour, salt, baking powder, sugar and poppy seeds. Combine eggs, oil, milk and flavorings. Add to dry ingredients and mix well. Bake in 6 greased and floured 3 x 5 inch mini loaf pans for 45 minutes at 350 degrees. Will be done when toothpick inserted in center comes out clean.

GLAZE

¼ cup orange juice
¾ cup sugar
½ tsp each: almond, vanilla, butter flavorings

Combine ingredients and spoon over slightly cooled bread. This is a very moist and sweet bread.

ANGEL BISCUITS

5 cups flour
1 pkg. yeast
2 Tbsp. warm water
1 tsp. baking soda

2 Tbsp. sugar
1 ½ tsp. salt
1 cup vegetable shortening
2 cups buttermilk

Dissolve yeast in warm water. Sift dry ingredients into bowl. Cut in shortening. Add buttermilk, then yeast. Stir until thoroughly moistened. Turn out on floured board and knead for 2 minutes. No rising required. Roll to ¼ inch thickness and cut into 1 ½ inch rounds. Brush with melted butter.

Bake on ungreased pan in 400 degree oven for 12 - 15 minutes until slightly browned. These are delicious served with a slice of country ham.

PUFFS

1 cup water
½ cup margarine or butter
1 cup flour
4 eggs

Heat oven to 400 degrees. In saucepan, heat water and butter to a rolling boil. Stir in flour. Stir vigorously over low heat until mixture forms a ball, about 1 minute. Remove from heat. Beat in eggs all at once until smooth and glossy (very important step). Drop dough by slightly rounded teaspoonfuls onto ungreased baking sheet. Bake 25 minutes until puffed. Cool on wire rack away from drafts. May be frozen. Cut off tops of puffs. Remove filaments of soft dough. Fill.

Open House

The following recipes were served at the 1983 Carnton Open House and were provided by volunteers of the association.

CHEESE STICKS

½ lb. mild cheddar cheese
½ lb. sharp cheddar cheese
1 stick butter
2 cups flour
1 tsp. salt
½ tsp. cayenne pepper

Cream butter, add grated cheese and the rest of the ingredients. Run through the star of a cookie press. Bake at 350 degrees for 20 minutes, or until firm and slightly brown.

CREAM PUFFS

½ cup butter
1 cup boiling water
1 cup enriched flour
¼ tsp. salt
4 eggs

Melt butter in water. Add flour and salt all at once. Stir vigorously. Cook, stirring constantly until mixture forms ball that does not separate. Remove from heat and cool slightly. Add eggs, one at a time, beating vigorously after each addition until mixture is smooth. Drop dough balls the size of a teaspoon two inches apart on a greased baking sheet. Bake for 15 minutes at 450 degrees. Reduce heat to 325 degrees and bake 25 minutes longer. When cool, fill with sweetened whipped cream.

PECAN TASSIES

PASTRY

1 - 3 oz. pkg. cream cheese
½ cup margarine
1 ½ cups flour, sifted

Let cream cheese and margarine soften to room temperature. Blend and stir in flour. Chill about one hour. Divide into three dozen balls. Place in ungreased miniature size muffin cups. Press dough against bottom and sides of cups.

FILLING

1 egg
1 cup light brown sugar
1 Tbsp. margarine

1 tsp. vanilla extract
1 cup pecans, chopped

Beat egg, sugar, margarine, vanilla and a pinch of salt together until smooth. Divide half of the pecans among the pastry lined cups. Add egg mixture and top with the rest of the pecans. Bake at 350 degrees for about 25 minutes or until filling is set. Cool and remove from muffin pans. These freeze well ahead of time.

CHOCOLATE PIE

3 eggs
1 cup sugar
½ cup cream
1 Tbsp. cocoa

2 Tbsp. flour
1 Tbsp. butter
1 tsp. vanilla extract

Separate eggs. Mix together sugar, cocoa, and flour. Add cream, butter and vanilla extract. Cook this over low heat until it begins to thicken. When cool, add slightly beaten eggs yolks. Pour mixture into a pie shell that has been baked ¾ of the way done. Bake until mixture is set. Beat egg whites, adding 6 tablespoons sugar. Put meringue on top and bake until slightly brown.

Thanksgiving or Christmas Dinner

ROAST TURKEY

I have used this Craig Claiborne recipe from Bon Appetit magazine *since 1980. It is nearly foolproof. The turkey is always beautifully brown, tender and juicy.*

16 to 20 servings

1 - 20 pound turkey, fresh; neck and giblets reserved
8 or 9 cups cornbread stuffing
4 Tbsp. peanut, vegetable or corn oil
1 lge. onion, chopped
Salt and freshly ground pepper
2 cups water
1 cup turkey or chicken broth

Preheat oven to 375 degrees. Fill turkey cavity with stuffing; push tail of turkey inside cavity to secure stuffing.

Coat bottom of shallow roasting pan with 1 tablespoon oil.

Set turkey breast side up in pan. Add turkey neck and onion to pan. Rub entire surface of turkey with remaining 3 tablespoons oil. Sprinkle with salt and pepper.

Roast, basting frequently with pan juices, until turkey is golden brown, about 45 to 60 minutes. Reduce oven temperature to 350 degrees. Tent turkey loosely with foil and continue roasting 1 hour, basting often.

Reduce oven temperature to 325 degrees. Add 1 cup water to pan. Continue roasting for 1 hour, basting frequently. Add broth and continue roasting until the turkey tests done.

Carve turkey at table or just before serving.

Vicki Stout

SARAH OWEN EWING'S DRESSING

Sarah Owen Ewing was a McGavock who lived at Riverside in Franklin. Sarah Ewing Parker Peay is her descendant and a long-time Carnton volunteer and supporter.

CORNBREAD (Make a day or two ahead.)

1 cup buttermilk
2 eggs, beaten
1 cup self-rising corn meal

Mix above ingredients and pour into bacon-greased, regular-sized black skillet which has been preheated in a 450 degree oven. Bake 20 minutes. Crumble together with 8 regular sized biscuits.

CHICKEN STOCK

3 chicken wings
3 chicken backs
3 chicken necks
2 Tbsp. butter
2 celery stalks

½ onion cut into pieces
Salt
Black pepper
Red pepper

Salt down overnight 3 chicken wings, backs and necks. Rinse lightly next day. Cook over medium heat with plenty of water, black and red pepper and pats of butter, celery and onion for 30 minutes after mixture is boiling.

3 big stalks celery, chopped
2 small onions, chopped
1 Tbsp. butter

1 tsp. poultry seasoning
Pinch of celery seed
Salt

Sauté above ingredients with butter in a little water for 20 minutes. Combine crumbled bread, celery, onion celery seed and poultry seasoning. Salt to taste. Add stock until very moist. Bake in casserole dish at 450 degrees about 30 minutes.

Sarah Ewing Parker Peay

MCGAVOCK FAMILY
CRYSTALIZED CRANBERRIES

This recipe was written in the hand of Miss Jennie Gant, a Franklin native who died several years ago. She added: "Served at Carnton during Thanksgiving and Christmas."

1 qt. cranberries
3 cups water
4 apples cut into squares
1 cup white raisins
3 cups sugar
1 tsp. almond flavoring

Cover cranberries with the water. Cook until they [cranberries] commence to pop. Add the apples and raisins. Add sugar, cook 5 minutes. When cool, add almond flavoring.

This keeps in refrigerator well.

SIMPLE CRANBERRY SAUCE

1 - 12 oz. bag fresh cranberries
1 cup sugar
1 cup water
2 ¼ tsp. finely grated orange peel
½ tsp. coarse kosher salt

Bring all ingredients to boil in heavy medium saucepan, stirring often. Reduce heat to medium-low and simmer until most of cranberries burst, stirring occasionally, about 10 minutes. Transfer sauce to medium bowl. Cool, cover and refrigerate cranberry sauce. Can be prepared up to one week ahead of time. Keep refrigerated.

Yvonne Thompson

Mrs Harock Family Crystalize
Cranberries served at Clinton
during Thanksgiving & Christmas
_____

1 qt. Cranberries cover with
3 cups water. Cook until th
commence to pop. add thery
4 apples cut into squares.
add 1 cups white raisens

3 cups sugar Cook 5 Minute
When cool add 1 teas almond
Flaving. This keeps in
refrigerator Well.

SWEET POTATO CASSEROLE

4 cups sweet potatoes, mashed
3 eggs, beaten
1 cup sugar
½ cup milk
1 stick butter, melted
¾ tsp. nutmeg
1 Tbsp. vanilla

Mix until creamy with electric mixer.

TOPPING

⅓ cup light brown sugar
⅓ cup self-rising flour
⅓ stick butter, room temperature
¾ cup pecans, chopped

Mix well until grainy. Sprinkle on top of sweet potatoes and bake at 350 degrees for approximately 35 to 45 minutes.

Jo Ann Yancy

PUMPKIN PIE

1 cup sugar
1 tsp. pumpkin pie spice
½ tsp. cinnamon
1 ½ cups canned pumpkin
1 large can undiluted evaporated milk
2 eggs

Mix filling until smooth. Pour into pie crust. Bake in 425 degree oven for 15 minutes. Then 350 degree oven for 35 minutes until knife comes out clean.

Patti Caprara

TURKEY HARVEST HOME

For over seventy years, beginning in the early twentieth century, the Hicks Family celebrated Harvest Home by inviting their neighbors over on the Saturday after Thanksgiving. It was an easy way to get rid of the Turkey leftovers.

1 ½ cups fresh mushrooms, sliced
1 cup carrots
1 cup frozen peas
½ cup yellow or green sweet pepper, chopped
¼ cup butter
⅓ cup all-purpose flour
¼ teaspoon ground sage
1 cup chicken stock
1 cup whole milk
2 cups cooked turkey, cubed
Whole-wheat biscuits

In a medium saucepan in a small amount of boiling water, cook mushrooms, carrots, peas, and pepper, covered, until the carrots are crisp-tender (5 - 7 minutes). Drain and set aside.

In a large saucepan melt the butter. Stir in the flour and sage. Add chicken broth and milk all at once. Cook and stir until thickened and bubbly; cook and stir two minutes more. Stir in carrot mixture and turkey; heat thoroughly. For each serving arrange two or three biscuits on a plate; spoon turkey mixture on top. Makes 6 servings.

Robert Hicks

Carnton Sunset Concert Picnic

The Carnton Sunset Concert series is a long-standing tradition in Williamson County. Each summer, Carnton presents three pop concerts on the lawn on the last Sunday of June, July and August. Patrons purchase food on site, or bring picnics such as this one, by a group of fabulous Franklin cooks.

TROPICAL FRUIT SALAD

6 cups fresh cut up fruits
(including pineapple, orange
sections, grapefruit sections,
bananas, and grapes)
½ cup macadamia nuts or
pecans, chopped

½ cup flaked coconut
8 oz. sour cream
¼ cup brown sugar
1 tsp. vanilla

In large bowl combine fruits, nuts, and coconut; toss together. In small bowl combine sour cream, sugar, and vanilla; stir to mix. Add sour cream to fruits and stir. Chill and serve.

Janet Frazier

DEVILED EGGS

We use pickles made by our mother Emeline Gist's recipe, but they are 15 days worth of trouble. I am sure any good sweet pickle will do.

Hard-cooked eggs
Mayonnaise
Mustard

Salt
Sweet pickles, chopped and
undrained

Use however many hard-cooked eggs you need for your group. Cut in half and place the yolks in a food processor. Add mayonnaise, mustard, salt and chopped sweet pickles with pickle juice to taste. Process until smooth.

Lucy Battle and Nancy Moody

145

OLIVE CHEESE PUFFS

½ lb. sharp cheddar cheese, grated
¼ lb. butter
¼ tsp. paprika
1 cup all-purpose flour, sifted
¼ tsp. salt
Dash of cayenne pepper
50 pimiento-stuffed olives, well drained

Preheat oven to 400 degrees.

Mix cheese and butter and beat until creamy. Add flour, salt, paprika, and cayenne. Mix well. Mold 1 tablespoon of dough around 1 olive.

Bake on an ungreased cookie sheet for 15 minutes.

Linda Patrick

TENNESSEE TOMATOES WITH BASIL DRESSING

3 - 4 tomatoes, peeled if desired
⅓ cup olive oil
¼ cup red wine vinegar
1 tsp. salt
¼ tsp. pepper
1 garlic clove, pressed
1 Tbsp. chopped parsley
Chopped fresh basil or 1 tsp. dried whole basil
¼ cup Vidalia onion, chopped

Cut tomatoes into ½ inch thick slices and arrange in a large shallow dish. Set aside. Combine remaining ingredients in jar, cover tightly and shake. Pour over tomato slices.

Cover and marinate in refrigerator several hours.

Lucy Battle

SWEET and SOUR ASPARAGUS

1 can green asparagus spears
⅓ cup red wine vinegar
¼ cup sugar
¼ cup water
½ tsp. salt
3 - 6 whole cloves
1 stick cinnamon
¼ tsp. celery seed

Drain asparagus and put in an 8 x 8 Pyrex dish. Bring rest of ingredients to boil and pour over drained asparagus while hot. When cool refrigerate for 2 days. Drain and serve cold.

Margaret Roberts

SHRIMP and PASTA SALAD

2 cups buttermilk
2 cups mayonnaise
2 pkgs. Buttermilk Ranch
dressing mix (2 oz. each)
1 lb. vermicelli spaghetti
½ cup green pepper, chopped
2 cups celery, chopped

10 - 12 green onions, chopped
3 hard-cooked eggs, chopped
1 - 2 oz. jar diced pimento
⅔ cup almonds, sliced and
toasted
2 lbs. uncooked, unpeeled
shrimp

Mix buttermilk and mayonnaise with ranch dressing mix according to package directions. Break spaghetti in pieces and boil until tender. Drain. While hot, mix in the green pepper, celery, green onions, hard-cooked eggs, and pimento; refrigerate overnight.

Add shrimp to boiling salted water and cook just until cooked through, about 3 minutes. Immediately drain shrimp in colander and immerse in ice and water to stop cooking. Cool completely. Drain well. Peel and devein shrimp. Add shrimp and almonds to pasta mixture just before serving.

Susan Williams

HOMEMADE PEACH ICE CREAM

1 qt. whole milk
2 ¾ cups sugar, divided use
¼ cup all-purpose flour
½ tsp. salt
4 eggs, slightly beaten
1 Tbsp. vanilla
3 cups light cream (half and half)
1 qt. fresh peaches, peeled and diced

Scald milk in the microwave, about 5 minutes or until bubbles begin to form around the edge. In separate bowl, mix 2 cups of the sugar, flour and salt. Add enough hot milk to sugar-flour mixture to make a thin paste. Stir paste into hot milk and return to the microwave; cook till it thickens slightly, 5 - 7 minutes.

Add hot mixture gradually to beaten eggs and place back in microwave until thickened, about 2 minutes---watch carefully. Cool in refrigerator overnight.

When ready to freeze, add light cream and vanilla and place mixture in prepared ice cream maker and start to churn.

Peel and dice peaches; mix with remaining ¾ cup sugar. After ice cream has begun to freeze in ice cream freezer, take top off and add and peaches. Continue freezing according to manufacturers' directions.

Nancy Moody

Back Porch Shrimp Boil

Carnton Board member Tim Kearns has generously donated and prepared several shrimp boils served on the back porch of the historic house as a fundraiser for Carnton. Here's his recipe.

½ lb. shrimp per person- use the 21 - 25 count size shrimp
2 Italian sausages per person
2 half ears of corn per person
5 small red potatoes per person
3 large whole mushrooms per person
1 large onion, quartered
2 lemons, halved
1 whole garlic, peeled
1 small amount of cayenne pepper to taste
1 large can of Old Bay Seafood Seasoning
2 bottles of your favorite beer

This type of meal is meant to be fun and casual. The number of people you are serving will determine the size pot you'll need. I can cook for 4 in a 5 qt. pot, 10 in a 30 qt. pot and 25 in an 80 qt. pot (I use a boat oar to stir the 80 qt. pot). Having a pot the adequate size will allow for the ingredients to turn over in the boiling water and cook evenly.

I usually get the water boiling about 60 minutes before serving time. The smell of the seasonings in the steam gets people excited and hungry! You can make it spicier by adding cayenne pepper at this point. If I'm serving people whose tastes I don't know, I back off on the spice and let them add it themselves while they are eating. I add the Old Bay Seafood Seasoning, onion, garlic, lemons and two bottles of beer. Remember to keep extras in a cooler handy for the cook!

Cut the Italian sausage into bite-size pieces (approx 1 - 1 ½ in. lengths). I like using Italian sausage because it adds some additional flavor to the boil and it tastes good! Make sure the corn is thawed or it drops the temperature of the pot dramatically and stops the boiling. The shrimp can remain frozen until you drop them in the water.

About 30 minutes before you want to serve I start by putting the potatoes in the pot. They will take the longest to cook. Wait 10 minutes and add the corn, sausage and mushrooms. Wait 10 more minutes; check the potatoes to make sure they are getting soft by spearing them with a long fork. I try to test one of the biggest ones floating by, because if it is done the rest are done. When the potatoes are cooked you're ready for the shrimp. I generally don't cook them more than about 3 or 4 minutes. If the water is at a full boil, which it should be when you add them, cooking 4 minutes will cook them sufficiently and keep them from being tough.

The amount of ingredients may change depending on the crowd….if you have hungry guys you may want slightly more than ½ lb. per person or 2 Italian sausages or 2 baby corn ears per person. Serve with cocktail sauce, butter for the potatoes and hot sauce for those who want to "kick it up a notch." It creates an entire "fun" meal all in one pot.

Tim Kearns

Index of Recipes

BEVERAGES 14

APPETIZERS 22

SALADS 54

Bonnie's Strawberry Salad 62
Caesar Salad 58
Candie's Strawberry Salad 61
Chituna Salad 58
Crunchy Tuna Salad 59
Cuke-Onion Salad 55
Frozen Lemon Salad 57
German Potato Salad 55
Henny Penny Pasta Salad 63
Mississippi Tomato Aspic 57
Old Fashioned Macaroni Salad 64
Olive-Corn Mexicali Salad 63
Patti's Strawberry Spring Salad 61
Pear and Apple Salad 60
Potato and Green Bean Salad 56
Potato Salad 54
Spinach Salad 59
Sweet Broccoli Slaw 56
Sweet Sour Spinach Salad 60

MAIN COURSES 66

POULTRY 67

Baked Mustard Chicken 69
Chicken Almondzini 72
Chicken Cacciatore 68
Chicken Casuela 70
Chicken Croquettes 66
Chicken Loaf 67
Chicken Parisienne (Crock Pot Style) 73
Chicken Rollups 72
Company Chicken 69
Grilled Marinated Cornish Game Hens 71
Lemon Basil Grilled Chicken 68
Smoked Turkey Wraps 67

Sweet and Sour Chicken 70
Tuscan Chicken Cakes with Tomato-Basic Relish 74

PORK 75

Herbed Pork Roast 77
Kirk's Spare Ribs 75
Marinated Pork Tenderloin 78
Pork Chops a la Babette 76
Pulled Pork 75
Roast Pork Tenderloin 77
Stuffed Pork Chops 76

BEEF 79

Beef and Broccoli Pie 81
Chili Relleno Bake 79
Dried Beef in Sour Cream 82
Flank Steak 82
Molly's Meatloaf with Roasted Potatoes 81
Scotch Stew 80
Swiss Steak 80

SEAFOOD 83

BBQ Shrimp 84
Cajun Catfish with Pecan Crust 83
Ginger-Soy Marinade 88
Lisa's Crab Cakes 84
Oyster Spaghetti 87
Sarah Owen Ewing's Scalloped Oysters 83
Seafood Gumbo 86
Seared Salmon with Tomato, Leeks and Artichokes 89
Shrimp Jambalaya 88
Stuffed Shrimp 89

BREAKFAST CASSEROLES 90

Breakfast Casserole 91

Ginger Cookies 114
Golden Lemon Butter 115
Italian Cream Cake 112
Kim's Chocolate Pie 128
Linda's Coconut Cake 114
Lilian Jackson Jomes's Pound Cake 113
Mattie Jackson's Best Lemon Ice Cream 110
Mattie Jackson Hicks's Mother's Boiled Custard 118
Mattie Jackson Hicks's Mother of all Chess Pies 113
Molasses Cookies 122
Mom's Sugar Cookies 126
Nany's Buttermilk Pound Cake 111
Oreo Balls 127
Peach and Blueberry Crisp 116
Pecan Balls 110
Polly Hicks' Grandmother's Custard 121
Poorfarm Hollow Ice Cream 130
Poorfarm Hollow Jam Cake with Caramel Icing 129
Pumpkin Pie Bars 123
Shakertown Corn Pudding 123
Strawberry Pie 111
Sugar-Free Trifle 128
Verna's Cheesecake 119
Transparent Pudding 108
Tutti-Fruity Homemade Ice Cream 115
Walnut Balls 125

SPECIAL MENUS 132

HIGH TEA 132

Angel Biscuits 135
Bourbon Fruit Rolls 132
Cucumber Sandwiches 133
Fudge 133
Hot Chicken Salad 133
Poppyseed Bread 135
Puffs 135